This book is dedicated to my dearest husband Owen and my dearest sister Helen. I thank them both for their continued support during the writing of this book.

MY LIFE IN AND OUT OF THE SAND DUNES

CONTENTS

CHAPTER 1 WHY?

Who would have thought it? Little ol' me re-locating to The Kingdom of Saudi Arabia to pursue different avenues, broaden my horizons, enlighten my life and hey, why not?

It was 1984 and I was 29. I was working at Kings College Dental Hospital, London as head nurse on the Primary Care department. I had been there for 3 years and had been given the opportunity to explore different avenues of dentistry that weren't available to me in General Practice. I was lucky enough to observe specialized procedures in theatre, performed by Oral surgeons but it didn't fulfil my hunger for travel. I wanted more out of life and there was a great big, wide world out there!

So, I applied for a job at The King Abdulaziz Armed Forces Hospital in Saudi Arabia, a Muslim country that was a far cry from the Christian background I had been brought up with.

Why Saudi Arabia you are probably asking? Being honest, the tax free salary was probably one of the biggest attractions. We all know how hard it is to save some money for holidays and running your own car. It's expensive and you end up taking on extra jobs to subsidise these luxuries. I always had a second job to make ends meet, so why not be adventurous and earn a better salary? I thought it a good idea to read up a little about this country and educate myself on some of its traditions and customs; it is well known that Saudi Arabia is a very conservative but intriguing country!

Saudi Arabia has many natural beauties and resources. It also has an arid climate with vast isolated areas which are home to beautiful valleys, landscapes and other wonders.

I will talk more about the traditions and customs throughout the book.

My application was sourced through a reputable recruiting company and I was invited to attend an interview and medical in London. Exciting and yes, I was offered a position at the 'King Abdulaziz Armed Forces Hospital'. I gave my notice in at 'Kings Dental Hospital' and went back to spend time with my parents in Bridgwater, Somerset and prepare for my new beginnings. It was sad leaving 'Kings'. I had gained a lot of experience there, made a lot of good friends and took opportunities to go to the theatre, the Ballet and see all the sights unique to London. A friend was able to obtain tickets for us to be part of the audience of the 'David Frost Show', which was satellited to Australia. The guests were 'Wham' and 'Raymond burr'. Raymond Burr was so big that he had to be given a special chair to sit in without arms. A 'prompter' would pass by the audience with a board telling them when to laugh and applaud. It was hilarious! I also went to see 'David Essex playing' Lord Byron, the poet. It was very funny as he kept forgetting which leg to limp on! My most memorable occasion was seeing my hero Rudolf Nureyev dance in 'Swan Lake', at the 'London Coliseum', twice! I found it 'awe inspiring'! The staff at kings bought me some very nice luggage as a leaving gift, so I was all set to go!

My parents were very apprehensive about my impending adventures, but I convinced them that it was an opportunity I wanted to pursue so they reluctantly accepted it.

Shopping for this adventure was interesting, as I had been advised to purchase garments that covered one's body very modestly, a far cry from western dress! So I purchased ankle length dresses, trousers and long sleeved tops.

I boarded the coach from Bridgwater with my parents looking up smiling through their concerned tears.

My sister Helen had gone through teacher training college in Eastbourne and was now married so my parents were now about to be distanced from their second daughter. I had been working in London for over 3 years but came home regularly. Helen still lived in Bridgwater and visited them often but it was still a wrench for them.

On arrival in London, I was met by a representative from the recruitment agency and joined a number of other people pursuing the same path as me. We were briefed on the customs of the country through video and literature and given 86 pounds to cover travel expenses. The next day, we boarded a British Airways Boeing 707 to begin the eight hour flight to Dhahran, Kingdom of Saudi Arabia.

CHAPTER 2 NEW BEGINNINGS DHAHRAN SAUDI ARABIA

My new life had begun!

Before entering Saudi Arabia, the company that employs you must obtain a work visa from the Saudi ministry of Foreign Affairs, which is stamped into your passport. They also advise you which inoculations are required, usually 'yellow fever'.

I arrived in the month of May so the first thing that hits you is the intense heat which can reach as high as 110 degrees during the summer months!

Once you have completed the 90 day probationary period the company sponsoring you must convert your visit visa into a residency permit or Iqama which is valid for one year, renewable. This permit is proof that you have permission to live and work in the Kingdom. You could be asked to show it at any time, especially if you need to open a bank account etc. When you want to leave/go on vacation, an exit/re-entry visa is required.

It was certainly an eye opener for someone who had only read or seen pictures of this intriguing country. I had visited Muslim countries before; Morocco and Tunisia but they didn't really compare to Saudi Arabia.

I was housed in an apartment block overlooking the Arabian Gulf with two other female expats. Mixed accommodation was not permitted, unless you were on a married contract. We had our own bedroom which allowed you your own space and privacy. I had a good relationship with my other two flatmates. Mandy was a fellow dental nurse and very self- assertive but unfortunately she kept 'budgies' that were very messy and noisy! Carol worked in the hospital's administration department and delighted us with her culinary delights, namely, curries. She'd been working in the hospital for a while so was able to offer all kinds of advice which was invaluable to us green expats. We shared some good times together but after a while I moved into a two bedroom with another friend, Vivian.

The Arabian Gulf was host to traditional, Arabic, sailing boats called 'dhows'. It was a very interesting way to travel and you could sail over to Bahrain, if you weren't in a hurry. Dhows have a raised hull and a sharp, pointed bow. They are made from wood and have a minimum of two triangular sails. Some have a single, large sail that facilitates easy sailing and provides excellent power to the boat. They also had traditional designs carved at various places on them. In olden times they were used for trading goods and fishing.

The expat community were very good at trying to keep life as normal as possible. I remember going to aerobic classes 3 times a week. The classes were held in the housing complex so I would put a jacket potato in the oven, just before the class and it would be ready to eat when I returned. Fancy remembering that! The classes were sweaty and energetic but exhilarating! There was also a swimming pool on the roof but during the summer months it was far too hot as it wasn't chilled.

The tower block was situated within a shopping centre which was very handy for essentials and takeaways! A firm favourite was grilled chicken, rice, pickles, salad and flatbreads. Other gastronomic delights were falafel sandwiches and shawarma. Falafel sandwiches are deep fried balls of mashed chick peas and spices, squashed down into an Arabic flatbread with tahini (a sauce made with sesame seeds), salad, pickles and sometimes chips, wrapped up like a giant sausage! Delicious! Shawarma are thin slices of chicken or lamb built very similarly, also in a flatbread. Also delicious! Other popular snacks included hummus, fool, tabbouleh and kibbe. The drink of choice in a restaurant was 'Saudi champagne', a mixture of apple juice, sparkling water, sprigs of mint and lots of ice which was very refreshing!

Working and communicating with other nationalities can be challenging, intriguing, frustrating, entertaining but also interesting and in the end rewarding. The Dental clinic was staffed with a number of nationalities including Saudis and a variety of others from around the world. Many of them became good friends who I kept in touch with.

A phrase often used by Muslims was 'Inshallah', which translates to, 'if God wills' or 'God willing'. It's an Arabic language expression that comes from a Quranic command that commands Muslims to use it when speaking of future events. An example would be if you asked a patient to make another appointment, they would answer, Inshallah!

I was the assistant to Mona, an American Egyptian lady. She had a great sense of humour and was also a bit wacky, which is probably why we became good friends. I and some of the other staff would often socialise with her and her friends at weekends, as some of them worked on the American, military base where they served real alcohol!

An incident comes to mind whilst assisting Mona. She was in the middle of an extraction, a procedure that involves a great deal of strength and concentration. All of a sudden, out of the blue, popped a tooth, the wrong tooth! We looked at each other and burst into laughter! I think it was nervous laughter because we almost became hysterical! Luckily, the tooth was re-planted and the patient assured that all was well!

CHAPTER 3 FORBIDDEN FRUITS DRESS CODE AND CUSTOMS

The consumption of all pork products are forbidden (haram) in Islam unless, it is for survival. It is believed that Allah (God) knows what is best for his creation to eat. Actually, it is also forbidden to eat any meat that scavengers have already dined on or meat that was not 'Halal' slaughtered.

Halal slaughtering is based on Islamic law. The animal must be alive and healthy and the slaughtering must be performed by a Muslim. The animal's throat is cut in a single swipe so that the blood can drain from the carcass. (It is said that in the U.K. 88% are stunned beforehand by methods Muslims find religiously acceptable).

In relation to 'pigs', I must relate this amusing story that occurred in the clinic. As I explained, pigs in Islam are unacceptable. It was customary to have a number of small toys/gifts in the clinic to reward children for their good behaviour. In amongst these gifts were a number of different coloured, plastic pigs! They were given out to the children but with consequences! Some parents complained that they were offensive, so we were ordered, by the head of department, to remove them from the gift box! I have to admit that most of us found this extremely amusing so we gathered them up and scattered them on the Head of Department's desk (who was American). He wasn't amused but eventually saw the funny side!

Saudi television would not allow any words to be spoken relating to pigs or pork products. So if, for example, there was a cooking programme relating to pigs, the word would be 'blanked out', e.g. blank (pork) pie! It was very amusing but taken very seriously by the Saudi's.

CHAPTER 4 DRESS CODE

Dress code customs were educational to say the least. Ladies in general don't allow their faces or body shape to be shown. According to Raihan Ismail, lecturer in Middle East Politics and Islamic studies at the Australian National University, the dress code is open to interpretation. It has been shaped by centuries of cultures in different nations.

The Quaran, (the central religious text of Islam which Muslims believe to be a revelation from God (Allah)) calls for men and women to cover modestly. It does not actually say that you have to cover yourself in any particular manner.

Some will argue that it is a religious obligation, particularly the more conservative factions within the Muslim world. There are many variations and interpretations.

There are a number of head coverings:

The Burka: covers the entire body including the face with a mesh window to see out of.

The Niqab: covers the whole body including the face but not the eyes.

The Hijab: covers the hair and chest.

The Chador or Abaya: is a full length cloak held closed at the front by the wearer's hands or under their arms. Usually worn over other clothing e.g. jeans and top. This, in general is the chosen garment for Saudi ladies and for western ladies as well.

The Dupatta: is a long scarf draped across the head and shoulders, often accompanied by matching garments.

Some ladies are pressured into covering themselves from their husbands. Their cloaks were generally black. Depending on how religious they are, some ladies wear black gloves and socks for full coverage.

Dress code for western female staff at this hospital was far more liberal as we wore white trouser suits with three quarter length sleeves.

Men's traditional attire is an ankle length shirt called a 'thobe'. Generally white but can be beige or other earth colours during the winter months. It has a mandarin collar and is sometimes in the style of a western shirt collar. Long, white baggy pants, called 'sirwaal' are worn underneath. They also wear a traditional headdress that consists of 3 items. There is a large white or red and white checked square of cotton material called a 'ghutra'. It is folded diagonally into a triangle and placed on top of a white, small, skull cap called 'taqiyah', which is made of cotton and often embroidered, crocheted or knitted. that holds the 'ghutra' in place. The 'ghutra' is also held in place, on top by an 'igal'. The 'igal' is a two-loop coil of black, braided cord. It is heavy, course and the diameter is smaller than the head because it has to grip the 'gutra,' to prevent it from slipping from the centre of the head. The 'igal' was originally used to 'hobble' camels or cattle and was made of lightly woven black goat's hair and sheep wool.

The point of the head covering is protection from the sun and sand storms.

CHAPTER 5 CUSTOMS

Some ladies preferred to be treated by a female Dentist, even if their husbands were present. It was customary that some husbands would make the decision on what treatment their wife received!

Waiting rooms were segregated for males and females. If I went to call a patient for their appointment and they were praying, I would have to be respectful and wait!

When male children reach the age of puberty, anything between the ages of 9-12, they would be expected to sit with their fathers in the male only waiting room. Females reach puberty between the ages of 9 to 13 and can be married as early as 14. Segregation also applies to social gatherings, swimming pools and weddings. Restaurants cater for families by providing screens. I attended a few Saudi weddings because naturally, you build up friendships with the Saudi staff. It was an unforgettable experience. The males and females are in different rooms but that doesn't stop them partying and letting their hair down. The ladies love to dress-up and under their veils (if worn), their outfits, hair and makeup are stunning? I must add that there are some very beautiful ladies in The Middle East. They also love to include their ex-pat colleagues when the dancing begins! The less said about that the better!

They have this unique way of greeting/showing affection by cupping the top of their top lip and flapping their tongues up and down producing a high pitch warble. Amazing!

CHAPTER 6 SOCIAL LIFE EGYPT AND THE CAUSEWAY

The Social life in Dhahran was surprisingly good. You built up camaraderie between other ex-pats and organized events in each other's apartments. The drinking of alcohol is forbidden but where there's a will there's a way!

There are a lot of interesting sights to be seen in Saudi and sometimes trips were organised by the hospital.

One such trip was to the caves of 'Hofuf'. Hofuf is a city in the Al Hasa Oasis of the eastern region, 140km south west of Damman. The hills are made up of rocks like sandstorm and limestone which makes the mountains white. They are characterized by changing colours from white to light grey and have massive calcareous sandstones interbedded with soft reddish to yellow brown marvel clay. The caves are unique because they are tall and have a mushroom like rock formation. They are now accessible with walkways and iron railings inside.

There were plenty of excellent shopping malls to peruse but it was important that you were aware of the times of the prayer calls in the early evening because the shops would close during them. The final call could last for 20 minutes, which was a long time to be sat outside, especially in the summer months when the temperature would soar into the 100's, which was very uncomfortable. If you entered a restaurant just before the call, you were allowed to sit and wait, especially if the restaurant owner wasn't a Muslim.

I will go into more detail about Prayer calls later on.

Many of the stores stocked 'designer' clothing and other items which was a true shopper's paradise! There were also a lot of western stores and to name a few; M and S, Next and Debenhams. Of course, there were also the traditional 'souks' where you could buy anything from imitation watches, C.D's, clothing and household goods. I must point out that it was important that local customs be respected by western ladies by wearing the 'Abaya' and sometimes a hair covering depending on which souk you were in. If this was ignored and one was seen dressed inappropriately, there were religious police called 'Muttawa' (responsible for enforcing Islamic doctrine of Hisbah') who would ask you to respect their dress code by covering your body shape and head) I was never asked to cover my face as a western woman but sometimes my hair especially in areas dominated with local residents.

One of the attractions of working in The Middle East is the tax free salary. You were able to save a lot of money and contemplate vacations that were previously only dreamed of. My first vacation was taken soon after I arrived in Dharhan, a holiday called, Eid-Al-Fitr, which marks the end of the holy month of 'Ramadan'. I went to Egypt with one of my flatmates, Mandy. I had always dreamed of visiting Egypt but could never afford it. We booked ourselves into the 'Ramses Hilton' and I was ecstatic at being able to visit 'The Pyramids' and other historic sites! The museum in Cairo was unbelievable, filled with artefacts depicting life back then. You would have to spend a whole day there to see everything. I have to mention that Egyptian traders are a 'pest'! They are extremely persistent and annoying!

In 1986, 'The King Fahd Causeway' was opened. It stretches from Al-Khour, Khobar, Saudi Arabia to Al-Jasra, Bahrain. It is 15.5 miles long and a haven for people that wanted a quick fix of western hospitality!

Previous to the causeway being opened you would take a flight from Dhahran. It only took 5 minutes, so was one of the shortest but most expensive.

A friend and I decided to have a little weekend break, so took the opportunity, booked a flight and went across to Bahrain. We would go on a Thursday afternoon, return early on the Saturday and then go straight to work with suitcase in tow! The flight is so short that no sooner you are in the air; the plane begins its decent. Bahrain is a far cry from Saudi in terms of entertainment. There are a plethora of pubs and clubs serving alcoholic drinks and cocktails to die for! A lot of clubs in the hotels employ Filipino bands for entertainment. They are extremely talented and have the ability to imitate the real McCoy and they will oblige any request.

CHAPTER 7 FIRST TRIP HOME!

I was beginning to get excited as my first trip home was approaching. Having been in Saudi for 6 months I was missing my family and feeling very 'homesick'.

I couldn't wait to go shopping for those special gifts for my sister Helen, Rick her husband and mum and dad. I bought my mum a gold necklace, a Raymond Weil dress watch for my dad and gold earrings for Helen. I can't remember what I bought for Rick, but I do remember that nobody was left out.

My parents came and picked me up from Heathrow, laden with 'camp' coffee in a flask and egg and tongue sandwiches. I don't know why I remember that, it was just one of those things that will always stay with me, a happy and heart warming memory! I couldn't wait to see my friends back home and relate to them the experiences I had had.

CHAPTER 8 RAMADAN AND PRAYER CALLS

As Saudi Arabia is a Muslim country, the holy month of Ramadan is when healthy Muslims abstain (fast) from, eating, drinking and sexual relationships for 29/30 days, from dusk to dawn. They should also avoid becoming angry, swearing, fighting, immoral behaviour but, to show compassion. It is also the month according to Allah, (The Almighty) where the holy Quran (holy book) was revealed to the Prophet Muhammad, peace be upon him. The point of fasting is that it develops God consciousness, self control and health improvement by reducing/eliminating impurities from the body and to become and aware of the trouble of the poor, sick and hungry. It is a very joyous month for Muslims as they enjoy extra prayers and cleansing of the body. Fasting usually begins when the child has undergone puberty. Younger children can be introduced to fasting by doing it part-time.

There may be reasons for people being exempt from fasting: The elderly and the chronically ill, (including diabetics), women who are pregnant and breast feeding and travellers. If a woman begins menstruating in Ramadan, her fast has been broken and she will be expected to make up the time at a later date. This also applies to travellers.

If time can't be made up, that person should pay for another to be fed. This is known as 'Fidyah'.

'Kaffarah', means penance. If somebody deliberately misses or breaks their fast they should compensate by fasting for 60 days continuously or pay to feed 60 poor people.

'Ramadan Kareem' is the greeting used at the beginning of the month of Ramadan. It means,' Ramadan is generous'. Sometimes, Ramadan Mubarak is also used which means, 'Ramadan the Blessed month'.

Eid al-Fitr is the festival of 'Breaking the fast', the religious holiday that marks the end of the month long, dawn to sunset fasting of Ramadan, celebrated by Muslims worldwide.

Eid al-Adha is the festival of sacrifice in commemoration of the sacrifices of Abraham and his family. Muslims throughout the world celebrate this marking the end of their pilgrimage.

The working hours in the dental clinic changed during Ramadan, as according to Islamic law, Muslims aren't permitted to have certain procedures performed that involve liquid going in or coming out of the body during daylight hours, so it was open from 10 a.m. until midnight. We would work a morning/afternoon or an afternoon/evening shift for that month.

Although preventative dental procedures (restorations, scaling and extractions) do not invalidate fasting, a lot of Muslims prefer to have treatment after 'Iftar' due to personal differences in their views.

Patients who require emergency treatment are at risk of breaking their fast. If possible, a lot of Muslims prefer to delay or reschedule their treatment.

Oral medications are not permitted when fasting unless it causes harm or becomes life threatening.

Having talked about Ramadan, I feel that Prayer calls should be mentioned, as they play a prominent part in a Muslims life.

In Islam, Muslims are called to Prayer five scheduled times a day by an announcement which is called the Adhan. This announcement is called out from the Mosque by the Muezzin (a man) who stands either in the Mosques minaret tower or in a side door, depending on the size of the Mosque.

There are five prayer calls which are dictated by the position of the sun. Prayer demonstrates a Muslim's faithfulness every day. The five calls

are:

Fajr: performed before sunrise.

Dhuhr: performed shortly after noon

Asr: performed late afternoon

Maghrib: performed just after the sun goes down

Isha: performed before going to bed

Having talked about Prayer calls it would be remiss of me not to mention The Five Pillars of Faith of which Prayer is one and the most visible. The other four are:

Hajj: A pilgrimage to Makkah, (Islam's most holy site where only Muslims are permitted) that must be made at least once in a lifetime.

Sawn: fasting during Ramadan

Shahadah: reciting the Islamic profession of faith called The Kalimah

Zakat: giving to charity and aiding the poor.

CHAPTER 9 KENYA, GREECE AND THE FAR EAST

Mandy and I shared another vacation together in Kenya. She had also arranged to meet her mum there. We spent the first night in Nairobi and went to a well known restaurant called 'The Carnivore', which speaks for itself. Gigantic skewers of all kinds of meat were served. It was certainly an experience! Traditionally, Kenyans are known for a dish called 'ugali', a semi-hard cake made from maize and flour which usually accompanies meat stews and leafy vegetable stews.

The next day we went on a four day safari, travelling in an open jeep. The driver of the jeep was able to get quite close to a white rhinoceros which was a rare occurrence. We also witnessed hippo's wallowing in the most picturesque swamp that was draped with foliage with the sun's rays pushing their way through the leaves. I felt extremely lucky to have had the opportunity seeing all those beautiful animals in their natural environment.

One evening we stayed in the infamous 'Tree tops,' which was built on stilts. There was a bell in your room which would ring if any of the animals came to the 'water hole'. I was elated and privileged to witness a pride of lions that visited one evening. The restaurant was open air and attracted all sorts of 'creepy crawlies'! The floor of the restaurant was covered with giant beetles so during the meal I wouldn't put my feet down in fear of them crawling up my legs! After the safari, I went to Mombasa for a few days and rented a chalet on the beach. I am happy to say that I didn't come across any beasties whilst I was there. It was idyllic! The beach was beautiful and the sea, cool and blue. I purchased some unique, hand carved animals and African 'batiks' for myself and for gifts. After Mombasa, I flew home for a week. Those creepy crawlies must have gotten to me because I had a 'jippy' tummy and spent a lot of time in the 'smallest room'! My mum thought it was hilarious!

My mum was desperate to come out and visit me but it wasn't possible. Back in the 1980's my position as a dental nurse didn't warrant an application for a visit visa, even for a family member. She found it very hard to comprehend but those were the rules.

I was also lucky enough to visit Athens in Greece with another friend Vivian, the flatmate I shared with after Mandy. We met her mum there and found that the city had some very interesting sights and places to visit. One of the most famous is the 'Changing of The Guard', which takes place at the Greek tomb of 'The Unknown Soldier' and the 'Presidential Mansion'. The soldiers who perform this are a ceremonial unit that also guards the tomb. They wear very distinguished white jackets, wide skirts and Albanian-type slippers with turned-up, tufted toes.

Traditional Greek food is very popular in the U.K. especially 'Moussaka' which is layers of minced lamb, onions, aubergine, spices and a white sauce topped with cheese. Other gastronomic delights are; 'Kefdedes', which are vegetable patties, souvlaki, grilled meat wrapped in a flat bread with spices and yogurt, octopus, feta cheese pie with spinach, yogurt and olives.

A group of us decided to take a trip to The Far East namely Thailand, Singapore and Hong Kong. For one reason or another, everybody dropped out, so I decided to go on my own! My first port of call was Bangkok, Thailand. What a diverse city! Everything and anything goes! It has a lot to offer in terms of tradition, culture, shopping and well, use your imagination! Purchasing 'fake' merchandise is a 'must' and very popular. You could buy a fake Rolex watch for a nominal sum and impress all your friends! I bought one for my dad and it looked like the real McCoy! Apparently, the way to tell if it's real, is that the second hand 'sweeps', where as with the fake ones it 'jerks'! The battery ran out so my dad took it to a friend's jewellery shop to get it renewed. The jeweller didn't want to touch it in case he damaged it! My dad explained where it had come from so he reluctantly replaced it.

There are many places of interest. I was lucky enough to visit a centre that gave an insight of what Thailand represents; traditional dancing, elephants working and bathing and a traditional wedding. It was a wonderful experience and ticked all the boxes. The traditional mode of transport in Thailand is the 'Tuk-tuk'. It is also one of the quickest, easiest and cheapest ways to get from A to B. It is described as a motorized 'rickshaw' with 3 wheels, which can carry 2-3 passengers who sit on a bench.

There are many 'Buddahs' and temples to visit; The Grand Palace which has been The King's of Siam residence since 1782, Wat Arun, a Buddhist Temple, The Golden, Emerald and reclining Buddha's.

I took an internal flight and went to the north of Thailand, 'Chieng Mai', where I experienced a ride on an elephant at the 'elephant jungle'. I have to tell you that elephants are ultimately one of my favourite animals. I visited a heritage centre that sold traditional Thai, paper, bamboo, decorative (parasols) umbrellas in all colours. They were exquisite and of course, I had to have one! They made unique gifts and you could sit and watch the ladies painting beautiful designs on them. It was very artistic and skilful! They would paint a design on anything, so one of the ladies painted a design on my camera case.

The 'floating' food market literally 'floats your boat' and it's incredible to see all those vendors crammed together in their boats competing to sell their produce.

I wasn't that enamoured with Singapore, I found it too concrete and clinical. The streets are exceptionally clean as littering is a fineable offence.

It was 1997 and the British weren't in favour in Hong Kong at that time, because Britain was handing it back to China after a 99 year lease. It was sometimes difficult getting assistance as some of the Hong Kongese citizens didn't want to oblige the British. Having said that, it didn't really spoil my visit, I even took a ferry over to Macau, China for a day. China boasts a very rich cultural heritage and a lot was packed into one day. Part of the tour took us to a house that 'Michael Jackson' had visited. The lady of the house had taken his photo and he had signed it. We were also taken to a heritage centre where I bought Jacob, my nephew, a panda, cuddly toy! I met a variety of people but because I was travelling on my own, I spent most evenings in my room. On this particular evening, I saw a film advertised called 'Planes, Trains and Automobiles', staring Steve Martin and John Candy, so decided to watch it. Well, I laughed and laughed and laughed! I'm sure the guests in the adjoining room could hear me but I didn't care, it was hilarious! I bought some stunning gifts to take home including jewellery, silk pyjamas and traditional arts and crafts.

I was able to bring a 'Bonsai ' tree back from Thailand which I gave to my mum. She nurtured it and it flourished for many years. It was a phenomenal vacation, even on my own.

I made a lot of friends in Dhahran but after 18 months a friend Vivian and I decided to spread our wings so we applied for a position in Jeddah at 'The King Fahd Armed Forces Hospital'.

CHAPTER 10 JEDDAH 1986

So, good-byes were said and we headed off on our next adventure!

Jeddah was the pinnacle of my life because that is where I met my dear husband Owen which paved the way for the rest of my life!!

Jeddah lies on the coast line of The Red Sea. The accommodation was in a building called 'White Towers'. I shared with two other ex-pats and we became good friends. It wasn't the most salubrious of housing but as an added bonus, there was a swimming pool, a most welcome addition, especially when the temperatures soured to the 100's and over in the summer months. A television was provided but English channels were far and few between as satellite TV wasn't around then. We would arrive back in 'White Towers at 5.30 and look forward to watching 'The Muppet' show at 6-o-clock. How sad but wait! 'All Creatures Great and Small' was on afterwards! We had great girly nights. Some of us would cook; we would play music, bitch about men and have a blast! There was another housing complex where some of the girls lived, so we would take it in turns to visit each other. This housing was nicer in terms of the building and furnishings but it didn't have a swimming pool and not as well appointed. Taxis were easily available and cheap but not very well maintained! The air-conditioning didn't usually work and were only driven by men as women weren't allowed to drive! You would also find that they liked to play Arabic music, as if trying to prove a point!

There was public transport but ladies had to sit at the back, behind a partition and use a different entrance. It was free for ladies so that no contact was made with the male driver. I did use it once, just for the experience!

There was a curfew of 11pm if you ventured out at night. The building was manned with 24 hour guards who were all extremely obliging if you were a bit late!

Transportation was provided to and fro the hospital and for shopping.

There were a number of activities in the shopping malls including ice skating, cinemas and eateries. A group of us would go ice skating on a Monday night as mixed company was accepted for westerners.

As in The King Abdulaziz, the King Fahd dental clinic was also staffed with a variety of nationalities which I found fascinating as it was interesting learning about other cultures.

The hospital owned a beach cabin on the Red Sea so on a Thursday, as it was a half day, we would go on the transport provided and stay until early evening. (The weekends were Thursdays and Fridays). There was also a café there so lunch was catered for. It was fabulous and a great way to unwind. There was also a swimming pool on the hospital grounds that we used sometimes during our lunch break if it was a female time.

There were a lot more male and female expats in this clinic so my friend and I made a lot more friends and had some great times together.

The story I'm about to relate to you has to epitomise the height of male chauvinism, laziness and arrogance! I was assisting a dentist who was instructing a patient on oral hygiene care and how to floss his teeth. The patient decided that this was a woman's job so asked the dentist if it was ok for his wife to do! The dentist was a 'no nonsense' guy from Texas, who didn't take kindly to idiots! I think my jaw dropped a mile and the dentist, quite politely, through gritted teeth, suggested that it would be easier for him to do it himself!

I worked with a lot of dentists in the clinic but one of my favourites was an English guy, Bernard, from the Midlands. He had a big character and his family were very 'down to earth'. Before his family came out he would 'party' with us, dancing on tables and being one of the gang. But, I must say, he was very protective of us girlies'. My father had a stroke whilst I was there so Bernard took me under his wing. I was sad when he left but we kept in touch for a while. Hi Bernard, if you're reading this!

Four of my friends had met some American military guys and been invited to a July 4th ball at the American Consulate. I also got an invite and was very excited as it was a 'dressy' affair. I had a little 'pink' number and I borrowed a pair of very high heels from my friend Carol. Another friend Lynn did my hair and we all looked, well, 'gorgeous'! It was a fabulous evening with good food, good music, dancing, great company and of course liquid refreshment! The men looked 'dapper' in their 'dress' uniforms and were extremely respectful. There was only one drawback! Those shoes were killing' me! OMG! How did Carol walk in those things all night? I just had to take them off! Ohh, what a relief it was!

I was especially interested in 'Oral surgery' and luckily enough there was an extremely experienced oral surgeon at the clinic. Bill was British and his wife Inga, who was Swedish, was a hygienist. Bill's nurse, Sandra was Australian and we became very good friends. I would go and observe Bill as often as I could to keep my hands in. Digging out impacted wisdom teeth and repositioning jaws were just up my street! If Sandra was on vacation, I would ask to assist him.

There was an excellent team of lab technicians of various nationalities who constructed the dentures, crowns and other prosthetics. I became good friends with Ian and his girlfriend Linda, who were Scottish. Linda worked in the 'crèche' as a nursery nurse.

In the 1980's, ex-pats could have a Saudi marriage at the 'Sharia court. It was only legal in Saudi but for a lot of couples it was a great solution to be able to live together. Ian and Linda were able to do this and made a lovely home together. Sharia (Saudi) law has since changed and it is no longer possible for expats to be married this way. The only legal way to get married in Saudi is at the Embassy or Consulate.

CHAPTER 11 THE CORAL REEF

Some friends and I had been invited to a compound called 'Northorp', which was situated near the 'creek'. It became a regular haunt of mine and I made a lot of friends there. Three of the guys had transformed their villa into a bar which I sometimes helped out with. It was almost like being at home!

A few of us would go to the beach and I heard how beautiful the coral reef was.

The Coral Reef in Jeddah has been described as an underwater tropical forest, as it is home to many species of fish and sea anemones. A few to mention are; clown fish, black surgeon, barracuda eels hammerheads and stingrays. There is also a lot that are fished commercially; Grouper, Nagil, a red grouper and Hamoor. The temperature of the sea stays generally between 29-37 degrees centigrade all year round, so it was very pleasant for swimming in.

I fancied the idea of going snorkelling but, to be honest I was a little bit apprehensive about swimming over the reef because there is quite a steep drop. It can drop from 5-30ft and I get a little bit nervous if my feet aren't touching the bottom. I mentioned to two of my friends that I would like to have a go but also about my apprehensions. They suggested that they swim each side of me as we go over the reef. So, that's what happened and it was awesome! I can't put into words the beauty underneath the sea. It felt as if I had entered another world and I couldn't wait to write to my parents and tell them.

I would ring my parents every week from a pay phone over in the main hospital. The accounts office stocked one riyal coins and I would purchase 100, which was about 20 pounds. The personnel that worked there got used to me going over and usually had them ready for me.

I had been given the opportunity to work in the O.R. (theatre) in the main hospital, assisting in procedures that I hadn't done before. One procedure in particular sticks in my mind, as it concerned a five year old child. The child's parents constantly gave her sweets and sugary drinks, which resulted in that she had to have all her milk (baby) teeth removed, due to rampant caries (decay). The father of the child turned out to be the anaesthetist! Oh dear! He thought he was being a good father by giving her all those sugary treats.

My first vacation taken from Jeddah was to Turkey, with two friends at the hospital, Viv and Phylis. We stayed in the diverse city of Istanbul and were constantly amazed at what it had to offer. There was so much to see and do; The Blue Mosque, The Topkapi Palace, The Bosphuros Bridge and the The Grand Bazaar where you can purchase every kind of curio, clothing, Turkish delight and leather goods. I bought a red leather jacket, skirt and trousers. The proprietor of the shop took the trousers up for me there and then. I also bought a leather brief case for my dad, ornamental brass slippers for my mum, because she loved brass trinkets, a leather hat for my brother in Law, Rick and a lot more. I was laden with gifts. Sampling the street food was a 'must' and a gastronomic delight. Popular snacks include; kofte, which are meatballs served in a wrap, kebabs; strips of meat, onion, salad, spices and maybe some hot sauce put into a pita bread. The traditional accompaniment would be 'Ayran', a mixture of yogurt, salt and water. If you have a sweet tooth this dessert will blow your mind and I absolutely love it! It's called 'Baklava'; layers of filo pastry that are filled with nuts then covered with honey or sugar syrup. OMG, I can taste it now!

The exchange rate at the time was incredible and you felt like a millionaire. This vacation was taken at another religious holiday called 'Hajj'. (I mentioned this briefly earlier on but will now go into more detail).

CHAPTER 12 HAJJ

The Hajj is the annual pilgrimage to 'Makkah', Saudi Arabia, which is the holiest city for Muslims. It is a mandatory, religious duty for all adult Muslims that must be carried out at least once in their lifetime as long as they are physically fit and financially capable. The word 'Hajj' means, 'heading to a place for the sake of visiting'. The 'Hajj is the fifth of the fundamental Muslim practices and institutions known as the five Pillars of Islam. The Pilgrimage rite begins on the 7th day of Dhu al–Hijjah (the last month of the Islamic year) and ends on the 12th day. When the pilgrim is about 6 miles from Mecca, he or she must enter the state of purity and holiness known as 'ihram' and dress in the ihram garments. For men, they consist of two white seamless sheets that are wrapped around the body, while women may wear sewn clothes. The pilgrims cut neither their hair nor their nails until the pilgrimage rite is over. They enter Makkah and walk seven times around the sacred shrine called the Kaʿbah, in the Great Mosque, kiss or touch the Black Stone (al-Ḥajar al-Aswad) in the Ka'bah and run seven times between the minor prominences of Mount Safa and Mount Marwa. On the 7th day of Dhu al-Hijjah, the pilgrims are reminded of their duties. At the 2nd stage of the ritual, which takes place between the 8th and 12th days of the month, the pilgrim visits the holy places outside Makkah, Jabal al-Rrahmah, Muzdalifah and Mina and sacrifices an animal in commemoration of Abraham's sacrifice. Male pilgrim's heads are usually shaved and female pilgrims remove a lock of hair. After throwing 7 stones at each of the 3 pillars at Mina on three successive days (the pillars exemplify various devils), the pilgrim returns to Mecca to perform the 'farewell', tawaf or circling of the Ka'bah before leaving the city.

About two million persons perform the hajj each year, and the rite serves as a unifying force in Islam by bringing followers of diverse background together in religious celebration. Once a believer has made the pilgrimage, he or she may add the title ḥājjī or ḥājjiyyah, respectively, to his or her name. The pilgrimage, if performed properly, is believed to wipe out previous sins for the sincere believer.

'Umrah' is sometimes considered 'the lesser' pilgrimage in that it is not compulsory but is still highly recommended. It is generally able to be completed in a few hours in comparison to 'Hajj', which may take a few days. It is not meant to be interpreted as a substitute for Hajj.

Umrah can be undertaken any time of the year whereas the Hajj pilgrimage has specific dates according to the Islamic, lunar calendar.

CHAPTER 13 PEOPLE, PRESIDENTS AND PERKS

One of the 'perks' working at the hospital was that they always needed blood. When you gave blood you were given two days off which was great if you just wanted a long and leisurely weekend or, you could tag them on to a holiday.

On one particular day in the clinic we were called to an early morning meeting and advised that we were expecting a VIP. This VIP turned out to be the former president of Uganda, Idi Amin, who was in exile in Saudi Arabia, as it was one of the few countries that allowed him to reside. We were asked to be respectful and not to engage into any discussion regarding his former duties! He arrived with a large entourage including his son who required treatment from a hygienist. She was very reluctant to treat him but was strongly advised that if she didn't, she would be dismissed! So, to save her job, she did.

I spent a long time being the assistant to a very nice Saudi Periodontist, Omar. Periodontics specialises in the treatment of gums and is a genre of dentistry that I also found very interesting, probably because some of the procedures could be quite gory and bloody! Omar and his family spent time in Canada to complete his speciality but when he and his family returned to Saudi Arabia the kids missed their way of life there and was always requesting to go back.

Omar was asked by one of the other male, Saudi dentists to remove a tooth from his 12 year old son. I handed him the local anaesthetic syringe and to my horror he injected the WRONG side! I tactfully tried to tell him but arrogance took over and he proceeded to remove the tooth! As soon as the procedure was over I just had to tell someone so I went and explained what had happened to another dentist who was a very good friend of his. She couldn't believe what I was telling her and proceeded to confront him on his actions! He was very remorseful and luckily, the boy's father was very understanding. The tooth was replanted as it was a permanent one and necessary for the development of teeth and their arrangement in the mouth. Hopefully, a lesson was learnt from this incident?

On one of my birthdays, he had bought me a beautiful gold necklace. The pendant was a hand holding the letter J. There are 4 diamonds on the J and 5 on the cuff of the hand. It's exquisite and I will cherish it forever.

Shopping in the 'souks' was an eye opener, especially the gold souks. There were hundreds of shops next to each other all dripping with modern, ornate

and traditional bangles, bracelets and other items of jewellery. The atmosphere and ambiance was electric with the Middle Eastern smells of spices and incense. We would just sit, have a shwarma and a fresh orange juice and watch the world go by. You could spend hours down there just in soaking up the culture.
There were many souks representing countries from all over the globe that sold all kinds of household items, clothes, spices, furniture and trinkets. You name it, you could buy it and it was fun 'haggling' over the price. You could pickup trinkets for peanuts! By the way, cashew nuts were also extremely cheap so I took them home as gifts by the sack load!

I would try and be original when choosing gifts for my family so, on one trip home I bought my dad a lute! He was a music teacher and I thought "what an apt gift"! He loved it! My friend's brother in Bridgwater, was a professional guitar player and introduced my father and me to a guy who played the lute. He was very helpful and gave dad some useful tips on how to play it. Other authentic and unique gifts I took home were 'Arabic numbered' watches and clocks and alarm clocks that sang a 'Prayer call'! They were very popular and repeat requests were made from friends and family.

I was very lucky in that I was able to take a lot of my vacation time at Christmas. I remember arriving at Heathrow airport early morning; putting my luggage into 'left luggage', taking a tube into Oxford Street and then going to Marks and Spencer's to do some Christmas shopping. I would return to the airport, pick up my luggage and catch a coach home. One year I bought my parents 'sheepskin' coats. I hid them under two chairs in the dining room and pulled them out Christmas morning. My mum burst into tears. They couldn't believe their eyes!

There was an abundance of local and International restaurants but one of our favourites was a Moroccan restaurant down in the depths of the souk. It was extremely traditional and as in Morocco, we would sit on cushions on the floor and eat with our fingers from clay terrines and drink minted tea. I can't really explain how different this world was but it was exciting and I felt very privileged to be able to experience it.

My monthly salary was a check in Saudi Riyals, so I would go to a bank to change it into cash and then to a money changers to transfer the amount I wanted to send home. There would be separate lanes for ladies in the banks and actually, we were usually given preferential treatment. I remember later on, banks manned by ladies were introduced, which is what I call progress! There were plenty of money changers in the souk so friends and I would make a night of it!

CHAPTER 14 MUMMY DEAREST

In 1988 my mum became Ill. When it became apparent that she wasn't going to recover, I decided to return home to be with her and help my dad. Helen, my sister was having her second baby so had enough on her plate. Unfortunately my mum died so I stayed home for 4 months to support my dad. Whilst I was home I wanted to have something else to focus on so I found a couple of part-time jobs. I bumped into the technician that ran the prosthetics lab in the practice I had previously worked in and he offered me a job helping make moulds from the impressions of the patient's teeth. It was interesting to see another side of dentistry and actually help to construct the completed prosthesis. I also worked part time in a sports centre on the reception and in the bar. My sister's mother in law had a fabric and button stall in the local covered market which I helped out in on Saturdays. My goodness, you wouldn't believe the effort and trouble some people expected you to go too to find the exact button and for peanuts!

After the 4 months I decided to reapply for my old job at the King Fahd Hospital in Jeddah. To my delight I was accepted so returned in the March of 1991. I t was very difficult to say 'good-bye' to my dad, but it was time.

It was very exciting returning to Jeddah and rekindling old friendships especially with Owen, a special friend who later, became my husband.

CHAPTER 15 OWNY AND THEATRE GROUPS

Let me tell you how I met my husband.

Some friends had been invited to an evening of entertainment with a comedian. Owen, my now husband was working in the 'bar'. I had asked for a diet 7up and he made a comment that I didn't need a diet drink! I wasn't amused as he was with a past boyfriend who I didn't particularly want to see. Anyway, long story short. Owen and I became very good friends and eventually got married! More about that later!

The previous housing in 'White Towers' was adequate but the hospital had since rented accommodation on a compound called 'Sierra Village', which was part of Arabian Homes.' It was far superior to what we were used too, with swimming pools on every corner, a very well stocked supermarket, tennis courts, bowling alley, a very good restaurant and a function room which doubled as a theatre for the local expat theatre groups.

That brings me on to the theatre groups. Two of my loves in life are music and theatre, which probably stems from my father as he was a music teacher and became very involved in local music and theatre groups. I suppose being a proud welsh man from the valleys was a contributory factor.

I first became interested when I attended a performance of Die Fledermaus, performed by The Jeddah Light Opera at 'Jeddah Prep', (British school). I was impressed at the size of the orchestra and wanted to be part of it! JLO was headed by an ex-pat, Scottish dentist called Bill Scot. (Owen and I became very good friends with Bill and his wife Celia) After making some enquires, I was asked to 'come along' and join in! Oh! I forgot to mention that I played the violin, grade 6 in fact, but I hadn't played for a number of years. I was very nervous at the first rehearsal but the musical director and other musicians were very supportive and made me feel at ease. Dress code for the orchestra during performances was a white top and black skirt or trousers. I felt very proud wearing this attire with one of Owen's black dickey bows.

I had invited Owen to the after show party which was very entertaining as cast members would often perform small sketches and ditties! Owen was very impressed and made a comment that he would like to become involved! No sooner said, Bill Scott invited him to join the chorus of the next production which was, 'La belle Helene', (Music by Jacques Offenbach and words by Henri Meilhac and Ludovic Halevy) Owen gratefully accepted the offer and came along to rehearsals. 'La belle Helene' was performed at The Italian Embassy which was a wonderful venue to put on a production as it was outside and had a large stage and auditorium. So, whilst wer'e all in the dressing room, just before the production begins, Bill would go round and give everyone a spray of whiskey, for the throat of course! It was a fabulous tradition and very well received!

The leading man in this production became, let's say, 'too big for his boots', so a lesson had to be paid to bring him back down to earth! On the opening night, the leading lady, Helen 'blacked out' one of her front teeth, so that when she smiled at Paris (the leading man) his reaction and the audience's was one of complete surprise! Bill was not amused but it certainly created a sense of frivolous camaraderie!

I made a lot of new friends joining JLO and was elated that I had rekindled my love of the arts.

Owen and I continued to be involved in JLO productions; in fact, I became the chairperson a few years later. Although I thoroughly enjoyed playing my violin, I had a hankering to resume my acting abilities because I had completed a two year speech and drama course at Weston-super-Mare College and hadn't partook in any acting for a long time.

In one of the shopping malls, there was a very talented Filipino artist who was able to create a painting from a photograph. I had asked the musical director of a JLO production, to take a photo of me holding my violin and, wearing my black and white attire. I took it to the artist and he said it would take about 10 days. When I went to collect the finished painting, I was blown away! He had captured everything in detail, even down to the rosin on the bow and the pearl in my ring. I took it home as a gift for my parents and of course it took pride of place in the lounge.

The mall widely used in Jeddah was 'Jeddah International Market (JIM)'. It had a good supermarket that stocked a lot of western items, probably because the manager was British. One particular day, Owen and I were browsing in the 'sweety' section and noticed a box of chocolates that resembled 'liquors'! We cagily picked the box up and read the ingredients and there it was, alcohol! It sounds ridiculous, it wasn't as if we were desperate for a chocolate liquor, it was the fact that they were 'haram' (forbidden)! We felt like naughty children as we put four boxes into our trolley. We headed towards the checkout and the nerves set in. Were people watching us? Was it was a trap? We were paranoid! The cashier put them into our trolley and we headed out to the car.

Yes! They were in our grasp. We gave two boxes away as gifts which were very well recieved and gorged the other two ourselves! We went back a week later but there was no sign of them. They had obviously realized their mistake.

Owen and most expats would purchase 'out of date', non-alcoholic beer for making their home brews. It was cheap and usually, the sugar and yeast would be stacked next to it. The manager of the supermarket was British and a friend who would let Owen know when there was a load passed its sell by date!

We found that there were other groups that represented the Arts, two theatres and a choral society. Owen and I also joined both other theatre groups as they represented different genres from JLO. Although we didn't join 'The Hejaz chorus' we supported all their concerts, especially the Christmas ones as they captured the essence of Christmas and were mesmerizing. Actually, my claim to fame with the' Hejaz' is that I turned pages for the pianist, the musical director, at one concert.

The 'Hejaz' is a region in the west of Saudi Arabia. The western coastal escarpment is composed of two mountain ranges, the Hijaz Mountains to the north and the Asir Mountains farther south.

There was also the Hejaz railway, which was a narrow-gauge railway that ran from Damascus, to transport pilgrims to Medina in Saudi Arabia, where they would travel onto Mecca for the Muslim pilgrimage. It was completed in 1908 but severely damaged by Lawrence of Arabia and the Arab revolt during the First World War (1914-1918). Parts of the railway still exist and some of the sections are still functioning.

In the early days, many 'Off Runway players' productions were performed at a compound called 'Hoctief'. Hoctief was the construction Company involved in building Jeddah's new Airport, hence the name. It was a fabulous venue where they put on dinner theatres. There were tables for 8 people and you could bring your own, homemade 'juice'. It felt almost normal and was very popular with ex-pats.

It would be extremely remiss of me not to mention 'King Fahd's Fountain', which at 853 feet is reputed to be one of the tallest in the world. It is fed by saltwater from the Red Sea, which shoots a single plume of water into the sky. Visible across Jeddah, the fountain was completed in 1985 and donated to the city by King Fahd. The iconic landmark is visible from many vantage points, but remains most impressive when viewed from the shoreline, Corniche Street. From the water's edge you can see the sheer force of the single fountain jet which is illuminated at night.

Owen had a houseboy from Pakistan who came in to the kitchen whilst our very large turkey was defrosting for Christmas. When he saw the turkey, the expression on his face was 'priceless'! He had obviously never seen a turkey before and thought that it was a giant chicken! Quote, "Mr Owen, that is chicken"? Owen being Owen replied," Oh yes, this Scottish chicken" and proceeded to make a 'clucking' noise of a loud, strong, Scottish 'chicken' and then, much quieter and slower, a Saudi chicken, flapping his arms! It was hilarious!

We had shares in two beach cabins. One was called 'Blue Beach and the other, Silver Sands'. It was a nice way to relax at the weekends and be able to put on a swim suit. It wasn't possible or respectful to go on a public beach wearing a western swimsuit as it would be offensive to the Saudis and Islamic doctrines. Quite possibly, one would have been asked to cover up. The sea was the perfect temperature for swimming or just 'chilling' and we would just sit about, having bar-b-cues, and in the winter months build a fire, sing some songs and tell jokes. Occasionally, we would stay over as there was a room with A.C. if required. The cabins were such an asset as we would do a variety of activities with the other share holders. We even put on small 'skits', providing food and beverages. Some Fridays, a group would go on a 'five at five' (run 5kms at 5 o clock). It wasn't unusual for us to put on evening attire from the waist up if it was a special occasion. We looked ridiculous but it was fun!

We met a lovely Syrian man called Jo, who had a senior position with the Mercedes dealer in Jeddah. He had also come through cancer and so to give thanks, he would host a 'blast before you fast' party prior to Ramadan. Even though he was a Muslim, he liked to partake in a little 'tipple'! He had every kind of alcoholic drink you could imagine! What a treat for us! We certainly did have a 'blast' and was very grateful for his generosity.

CHAPTER 16 THE BURKINI

As I have already stated, Saudi (Muslim) ladies have to dress modestly and that especially applies to swimwear. I remember in the early days, they would go into the sea fully dressed which must have been extremely uncomfortable. An Australian Muslim lady, Aheda Zanetti recognised that there was a lack of appropriate attire for Muslim ladies to swim and exercise in, in public. She also responded to the 2005 'Cronulla' riots in Sydney, Australia. On the 4th of December, a small number of volunteer life savers were involved in a dispute with some young men of Middle Eastern descent that ended in a fight. The following weekend, thousands of racially non-Muslim Australians gathered and rioted at North Cronulla beach. Following the riots, 'Surf life saving Australia', assessed the situation and decided to recruit mixed gender, Muslim lifeguards. The Muslim ladies felt uncomfortable with western swimwear so, in 2007, Aheda designed a two- piece, yellow and red uniform that covered their head and body. This led to the design of the'burkini'.

The design of the 'burkini' is intended to be in accordance with Islamic tradition. It resembles a wet suit but looser and is made from finely knit polyester to make it lighter. Opinions differ by country and communities regarding the clinging material, suggesting that it shows the outline of the body. Some will argue that the head covering isn't long enough to cover the breasts and that there should be a skirt to cover their hips. It is a modest form that covers the whole body except the face, hands and feet although some ladies wish to cover their faces. The burkini consists of straight legged pants, a long sleeved tunic that is tied together so that the tunic does not float up when the swimmer is in the water. It also has a hood that can be separate or attached and sometimes a swim cap. Apart from modesty reasons, all religions have been seen wearing it as it acts as a protector from the sun and also worn by skin cancer survivors. In 2011, Nigella Lawson is known to have worn one in Australia to protect her from the sun.

Another production that has to be mentioned was 'Run for your Wife', performed by The Red Sea Players at 'Jeddah Prep'. It is a comedy and was written by Ray Cooney in 1983. It tells the story of a taxi driver, John Smith who juggles two lives, with two wives, who don't know about each other! John gets caught up in a mugging and wakes up in hospital with the wrong wife by his side and is forced to deal with explaining things to both wives and the police all at once! Owen played the taxi driver and I was one of the wives.

He had a huge speech to memorize which he delivered without hesitation every night. He received an enormous applause from a very appreciative audience.

Dinner theatres were also put on at the 'American Embassy' by the 'Off Runway Players'. Tickets were expensive because 'real' alcohol was served. As you can imagine, they were very popular.

Owen and I played the characters, 'Jack and Jill' in the pantomime 'Dick Whittington'. Quite boring parts really, not a lot to get your teeth into. In one scene, we were the only two on stage because we were in front of tabs, during a scene change. Owen got his words mixed up and caused a riot! Instead of saying, "I'll put a spell on you" he said, I'll put a SMELL on you! Well, as you can imagine, I lost it big time and burst into uncontrollable laughter! The audience's reaction was amazing; as they also collapsed into raptures of laughter! The classic 'man as dame' scenario was also unforgettable. Roger Whitby Smith, a rather eccentric gentleman was playing the 'dame' and had to wear a black, curly wig. As part of one of his scenes, a kerfuffle has to occur. During the kerfuffle, Mark, the other character involved (Mark), accidently pulled Roger's wig off! Off we went again, into raptures of laughter. (We actually think that Mark pulled it off on purpose to cause a ruckus)!

An unfortunate incident occurred when a character had to stamp on a note of money, as part of the scene. As we were in Saudi Arabia, a one riyal note was used. After the performance a complaint had been lodged, stating that it was disrespectful to stamp on the currency of the Kingdom. I had sold tickets to a Saudi lady member of staff who took her husband and children. I later found out that it was her husband that had made the complaint. After that incident, all members were asked not to sell tickets to Saudis!

I think it important to say, that the action involving the riyal note was not done maliciously but out of lack of knowledge of local customs.

CHAPTER 17 A ROAD TRIP

On one of the local religious holidays a group of us decided to go on a road trip to 'The Turkish Fort' and 'The Wahbah Crater'. There were nine of us (3 couples and a single man) travelling in 3, four wheel drives. We each had our responsibilities and were very excited about the expedition! We arranged to meet at a designated point to begin our 'convoy'! The route took us to the city of Ta'if, which is at an elevation of 1,879m on the slopes of the 'Sarawat Mountains'. Families of Baboons inhibit the hills and mountains near Ta'if and are a local attraction to tourists who feed them fruit and vegetables. It is quite frightening but exhilarating driving up the slopes of the mountains, which is called 'The Escarpment'. We stopped for a picnic lunch in Ta'if and reached our first stop, 'The Turkish Fort,' late afternoon. The remnants of the Fort are near rock carvings. According to legends, Laurence of Arabia fought on this site in 1917.We all decided to sleep in the four wheel drives but erected a 'Gazebo' as the sides acted as a 'mosquito' net. The bugs were rampant and we were very grateful for it. I cooked a beef stew which we heated up on a small calor gas stove accompanied with Arabic bread. It was decided that we all take a surprise, so we took ice cream in a cool box that plugged into the cigarette lighter. Somebody brought the game 'Trivial Pursuit' which was so much fun! The next day, John cooked beef bacon and fried eggs before we continued on our adventure!

The road leading to the 'Wahbah Crater' is old and bumpy but breathtaking and magnificent. It is off the beaten track so Owen let me drive for a few miles. I had a blast because I hadn't driven for a long while and I felt exhilarated and free! Wabha is a volcanic crater 250km (160 miles) from Ta'if on the western edge of the 'Harrat kishb' basalt plateau. It contains many volcanic cones and is 250 m deep (820ft) and 2km (1.2 miles) in diameter. The bottom of the crater is covered with white sodium phosphate crystals.

On arrival at the crater we set up camp in the lava flows. Six of the group decided to adventure down the crater which was arduous, long and not for the faint hearted, but apparently, well worth the effort. Not all of us felt that adventurous as the terrain was rough and it was pretty steep. John, who couldn't contemplate approaching the crater due to a severe fear of heights, remained at camp to prepare the bar-b-que. Once again, we played 'Trivial Pursuit' and the surprise of the evening was 'kinder eggs'. In the morning we had a gourmet meal of sausages and baked beans! It was an amazing trip spent with good friends and the opportunity to witness incredible experiences.

We also became members of the Caledonian Society due to Owen being Scottish. It was purely for social reasons as we had enough going on with the theatre groups. Owen was asked to join the committee but gracefully declined. A lot of the functions, especially 'Burns Night', 25th of January, (In honour of the poet, Robert Burns) were held at the British Consulate, which was a bonus as we were able to partake in a wee dram! It was impressive seeing the men in their traditional kilts, looking rugged and handsome! Our friend Ron was 'a Piper' and in attendance to 'pipe' in the guests. Traditional haggis was served and 'the address to the 'haggis' and the addresses to the lassies were read. A 'ceiledh' was in full swing and a band played to complete the entertainment.

We were very fortunate to be asked to a variety of events at the British and American Consulates because of the involvement and people we met through the theatre groups. We participated in 'carol' singing and functions to celebrate 'The Queen's birthday' at the 'British Consulate'. There were also 'pub' nights on a Thursday night and sometimes 'pork' products would be on sale!

Another production I must mention, performed with 'The Red Sea Players' is 'Stepping Out', by Richard Harris. This play was made into a film starring, Liza Minnelli and Julie Walters. It tells the story of an ex professional dancer, (Liza Minnelli) who opens an amateur dance class and then enters her students into a competition. It took 6 months for us to put it together because we had to learn some 'tap dance routines!' Yes! Not only did we have to learn how to do them well for the competition, we also had to pretend to do them badly, to show how we had improved as the show progressed. In the competition scene, we used props of top hats and canes. It was quite risqué as the ladies wore fish net tights and leotards! Owen was the only male with 8 women! There was this particular scene where he had to perform a 'movement' that can only be described as 'A windmill!' Try and imagine doing 'jumping jacks' and circling your arms at the same time! OMG, he got faster and faster every night and brought the house down! With live theatre, you can usually guarantee that lines will be forgotten. Even the greats, Laurence Olivia had blank moments. Well, in one scene, we all dried up and nobody said a thing! OMG, a second seems like an hour and it was a 'cringing' moment. All you want is for the ground to swallow you up! I kept thinking, somebody PLEASE say something! All of a sudden, I turned to Geoffrey (Owen), and blurted out, "What do you fink then Geoffrey?" (cockney accent). Poor Owen, I certainly put him on the spot! He managed to say something, thank god, which got us all got back on track. Oh! I must tell you this! We were all fitted with microphones, which are turned on when you step out from the wings onto the stage. Just before entering the stage the 'sound' man says the name of the character, then 'live!' A cast member, about to walk on stage suddenly broke wind! The poor sound man could hardly contain himself and the rest of us were busting! Poor women!

Omar, who I mentioned earlier, asked if he could purchase tickets for him and his wife. Oh dear! I didn't know what to say after being told that tickets weren't to be sold to Saudis, so I lied and said that they had all sold out! I felt awful! This was HIS country and I was embarrassed! He paused and went very quiet. I knew, that he knew I was lying, as he said to me, quote, "You can't sell me tickets, can you because I'm a Saudi?" I had to admit that that was the case and explained to him about the previous incident involving the Riyal note. He promised not to wear his thobe and that his wife would not wear an abaya. I felt humbled and thought to myself, Sod it! Who the hell am I to deny him those tickets? So, they came to the show and thoroughly enjoyed themselves. He came back stage after ward sand congratulated everyone on their performance.

I couldn't list the amount of productions we were involved in because there were too many, but we had a tremendous amount of fun and they were very well attended and appreciated by the ex-pat community. Once again, the camaraderie was incredible as every production involves a tremendous amount of work, not just from the actors but backstage, costumes, sound and light, hair and makeup.

CHAPTER 18 HUNGER PANGS AND CHICKEN

Oh! I must tell you this! It was the first day of Ramadan and I was assisting a very nice, young, Saudi, male dentist who was clearly suffering with hunger pangs. He made a comment and I responded by saying, "Oh, I'm sorry my wee lamb"! (Owen always calls me his 'wee lamb'). He quickly responded by saying, "Oh, don't mention food"! I felt awful and apologised profusely but he found it quite amusing.

I must also mention the staple 'takeaway 'of Jeddah, 'broast'. I could say that it resembles Kentucky fried chicken but the coating is far superior and crispier! It consisted of 3 pieces of chicken in the specially prepared coating, coleslaw, a bun, fries and garlic sauce. Unless you've tasted it, you wouldn't appreciate it.

The other 'fast' food we would buy was 'spit-roasted chicken, which came with a bag of delicious rice a, a delectable concoction of spiced, squashed potato, carrot and aubergine, a bag of pickled veggies and Arabic bread.

There were times when mixed parties were organised unbeknown by the authorities! It was important to be extremely careful otherwise you could be deported! A story that comes to mind involves my now husband. We had been ice-skating on a family night and decided to extend the evening at a friend's apartment that lived off compound. We had both partook in a liquid refreshment or two and on the way back from our friend's, were involved in an accident with another vehicle. Fortunately, a Saudi male stopped in his car, removed us from ours and took us to a hospital where we were taken care of by an Egyptian male doctor. The doctor shielded us from the police as they would have surely questioned our situation! A representative from the hospital came to see me and of course, questions were asked.

A very good friend of ours, Ali, came to the hospital on the evening of the accident after Owen had rang him explaining our predicament. He came with a load of cash that he had gotten from friends he was spending the evening with, just in case he had to bribe anyone not to inform the police that we weren't married! The next day he returned and took us back to Owen's compound, but drove like a maniac! He was crazy!

I consider myself very lucky that there were no underlying consequences and I was allowed to return back to work after one month as my left leg was put in plaster. Owen's right arm was also in plaster and luckily, his job wasn't put in jeopardy. I must add, the Saudi gentleman who had helped us, visited us in the hospital the next day and brought a bouquet of flowers. It was a selfless act of kindness that we will always be grateful for.

I was unfortunate to catch 'conjunctivitis' and had to take time off work as it's very contagious. My friend Norma, Ali's girlfriend, was staying next door, so invited me to go and have a coffee with her. As I entered the apartment she had the song, 'Bright eyes' on! We had a good laugh about it because my eyes were streaming and very itchy!

Owen and I were still supporting 'stookies '(plaster), when it was our friend John's, 40th birthday, so we decided to throw him a surprise party! One of his favourite meals was 'mince and tatties' (potatoes) so that's what we decided to cook, for 40 people! What a palaver! Owen's kitchen wasn't really up to it but we plodded on, browning mince and peeling potatoes despite the inconvenience of having my leg and his arm in plaster. We asked John's friend Brian to keep him away for the afternoon so that we could get everything organised and to return him early evening. But, when he brought him back, he was the 'worse for wear' and dressed in 'scrubs'! They had ended up at Brian's apartment 'drinking'! OMG! We were so mad because Brian knew about the surprise we had planned for John. Anyway, all went well, we all dressed up and a lovely evening was had by all.

Owen and his friend John ran the restaurant on the AAA compound which was open to the expat community. There was also a wooden skittle alley and bar which expat clubs hired for a variety of functions. There was the Golf club, Hash house harriers, Football and Rugby clubs plus numerous others. Each club brought their own 'happy juice' but the restaurant supplied food and soft drinks. We had a blast! Friends would ring Owen up and ask to work behind the bar because we had so much fun!

Owen and my relationship grew stronger and stronger and eventually we moved in together as we obtained a 'fake' marriage certificate.

We had a lot of 'gatherings' with friends, cooking, going to the pool and spending time in the Jacuzzi. Ali, our crazy, Turkish friend constructed the jacuzzi from a 30,000 litre fertilizer tank (unused) in the back garden. At weekends, Owen and Ali would go to a local petrol station and buy blocks of ice, the size of a large coffee table to cool it down. It could accommodate 8 people.

We had some friends round one afternoon and of course after a couple of hours things got a bit rowdy and out of hand! Our friend Ali decided that somebody should go into the Jacuzzi, whether they wanted to or not! My friend Julie was the chosen one but was not amused, as she was wearing a very expensive pair of 'Gucci' shoes! She obviously didn't have a change of clothes so went home wearing a pair of Owen's trousers and a white shirt! Unfortunately, Brian got stopped by the police on the way home, but when they saw how Julie was dressed, they were waved on!

Most Fridays a group of us would also go to the pool. On one particular occasion, Ian, a Scotsman from Fort William, had had enough sun and decided to go back to his house. On the way, he tripped over a sun bed. He picked himself up and continued to walk from the pool area. A couple of minutes later he returned, picked up the offending bed and threw it in the pool and said, "You won't do that to me again!" We all cracked up as Ian turned and walked away without saying another word.

Owen and John were asked to cater a 'wetting the baby's head' party. This party was for a senior work colleague of Owen and John's so it really had to be perfect! Margaret, Malcolm's wife had stated that she wanted EVERYTHING supplied including crockery, cutlery, glasses and ice. She also stated, in no uncertain terms, that everything was to be taken away at the end of the night! Owen and John set up mid afternoon and I arrived later. Owen was checking with John that he had brought enough ice, so John, quite indignantly, lifted the lid of a large cool box but slammed it shut immediately! He waited a second, cautiously re-opened it but slammed it shut again! It was a solid block! OMG. It was just like a 'Fawlty Towers' moment. John had delegated the task to 'Dress', the chef, who had just poured 5 gallons of water into a cool box and put it into the 'walk-in' freezer! Luckily, there was a garage nearby that sold bags of ice and Margaret and Malcolm were none the wiser!

As you already know, the consumption of alcohol is forbidden so if one is caught bringing it into the Kingdom, there are severe consequences! A male friend of mine, Chris, who worked in the main hospital, was caught trying to smuggle in a container of whiskey through the port. He believes that he was 'setup'! But who knows? He was given a long jail sentence. I can't remember how long it was but it was years!

Owen took myself and a friend to the jail to visit him and waited in the car. It was grim! We had to line up with the other ladies and children and go through what I can only describe as a cattle grid! Before entering the jail we were searched. I tried to take him in toothpaste and at that time a 'walkman' but everything was rejected. We would then be ushered into the 'yard' where carpets were laid out for us to sit on in the boiling, hot sun! Chris would come and sit with us on the carpet. But, listen to this! Owen would visit him but was taken into the governor's, air-conditioned office and given 'chi' (tea). Chris would be brought in to join them. Owen was also permitted to take him in some items and Chris was allowed to give Owen mail for his family. What's that famous saying? It's a man's world. At the end of Ramadan, a number of prisoners are 'pardoned' from their sentence as an act of humanity. Chris was one of those lucky ones but was deported immediately back to the U.K. He would never be permitted to return to Saudi Arabia again and was very lucky as it could have been a lot worse.

On the subject of 'forbidden fruits', friends of ours, Sue and Keith had invited us over for a bite to eat and drink, as they had gotten hold of some 'forbidden fruits', namely whiskey, vodka and ham! Whilst we were tucking into these tasty morsels my friend Sarah piped up and quote, "these tomatoes are lovely"! Well, as you can imagine we all looked at her and burst into laughter. The funniest thing was, she didn't realise what she had said, so I reminded her what we were eating and what she thought was the tastiest!

Our friends Ian and Linda, who lived on Arabian Homes, hosted a 'Murder Mystery' evening. They're great fun but you have to dress up as the character chosen for you by the hosts. Owen was given the part of a woman and I was given the part of a man! Owen got dressed in my apartment at Arabian Homes. He put socks in one of my bras to pad it out and we bought a pair of size 8 court shoes, a dress and wig. I put some make-up on him and he looked, well, what can I say, the part! I wore Owen's dinner suit, shoes and donned a moustache! Ian and Linda lived at the far side of Arabian Homes which meant we had to walk half way round the compound to reach their apartment. It was early evening and there were a lot of kids playing outside. When they saw us they began to follow! Owen was struggling in his heels and I started to howl! It was like 'the Pied Piper'. The trail of kids became bigger and bigger! It was hilarious! The evening was a great success and Owen's driver Nilo, came to pick us up. On the way back, Owen announced that he had to remove his bra! Nilo, being very respectful just gave Owen a strange look!

Thursday night was 'party' night and there was always something going on. On a huge compound called 'Dallah', ex-pats organised a night of, 'Battle of the bands'! It was a great night and there really was some talented musicians out there. We would dance and sing and, well, you know!

It was 1991 and Owen was going to be 41, so we decided to have a party in Ali's house. I decided to dress up as a belly dancer because a friend of mine had a fitting costume in red. It came with a veil, so Owen had no idea that it was me! I also wrote him a poem that went something like this:

Ode to Owny

I wanted to write this poem for you and I really hope that you don't have a clue,
You turn 41 today and I really have the need to say, that even though you work in parts, you are just a cuddly tart.
'Trust me', I hear you say, on this your very special day, but trust me my dearest friend, I'll be with you until the end.

CHAPTER 19 SHARBATLEY

In 1992 Owen moved to another compound called 'Sharbatley'. It was a very large compound with two Olympic size swimming pools, cafes, a supermarket and a fabulous restaurant that allowed you to take your 'homemade' juice!!

This compound is where we acquired our two Persian cats, a beautiful grey whom Owen named 'Princess' and a black one who I named 'Sam'. They were a joy! A friend's boss needed someone to look after them whilst he and his family were away on vacation! It transpired that their son was allergic to them and was looking for a more permanent home. Hey, after ten days there was no way those boo-boos were going anywhere!

They used to follow us to the supermarket and restaurant and patiently wait outside. They were adorable!

Owen and I made very good friends in 'Sharbatly', Mark and Dot. For some unknown reason, it was fashionable to decorate bottles with long, dripping candles of different colours and the more you used the more artistic it would become. Owen and Mark were very competitive and decided to see who could make the biggest! Of course, they both cheated by blowing on them to make them drip quicker and, stayed up all hours! But, there is a twist to this tale! Mark and Dot had a house girl who thought that the bottle needed 'cleaning', so scraped all the wax from the bottle and washed it! Oh dear! Mark was devastated but couldn't blame the house girl. Owen was delighted!

Owen and I travelled back to the U.K. for Christmas with our friends Mark and Dot. We landed at Terminal 2 and decided to have a coffee together as we all had some time before we had to catch our coaches. Dot and Mark left first so Owen and I decided to have a look in the CD shop, which was so close that I didn't bother to take my duffle bag with me, only my purse. When we returned, my bag had gone! I frantically looked around, but it was nowhere to be seen, so decided to ask the help of a security officer. I approached an 'Indian' man and explained what had happened. After a short pause he began nodding his head from side to side and then asked me, "What language are you speaking?" Well, as you can imagine, I just lost it and replied, "What language am I speaking? What language are you speaking"? I launched into an extremely angry and loud speech that I was born and bred in England. I was beginning to attract a crowd and Owen asked me to calm down which only made me worse! To cut a long story short and unbeknown to me, my bag had been removed by security as a precaution in case it was a bomb. I didn't know this until I arrived back in Bridgwater, when I rang the airport. I was asked to describe my bag in detail and thankfully they had it with all my important and personal items intact. They kept it for me until I returned to the airport as I wasn't in desperate need for anything. You can't imagine how relieved I was as everything was in there; passport, containing my exit/re-entry visa, money and jewellery.

During the 90's, Owen and I took a trip to Mexico. Whilst we were there, we took the opportunity to visit 'Chichen Itza', Mayan ruins of the Gods. It is one of the 'New Seven Wonders of the World'. It is a remarkable site which was founded approximately during the 6th century. 'Chichen Itza' means, 'at the edge of the well'. El Castillo, (the main pyramid) was built on top of another much older temple. Each of the four sides of the pyramid has 91 steps. The temple platform is the final step which in total is 365 steps which is equal to the number of days in the 'Haab' year. We were fortunate enough to be able to climb the pyramid because in 2006 it was closed to visitors as it was deemed unsafe. Funny story: The climb up was fine, but when we reached the top I began panicking about getting back down, as it was extremely steep and I had a fear of 'falling forward'! It was also raining so we were wearing black bin liners to keep us dry and I had a video camera round my neck. After taking pictures and a video we decided to go back down. Owen went first thinking that I was behind him, but I wasn't! I froze! I tried to think rationally because I knew that there wasn't any other way down but I needed more time to think about it! I must have lost track of time because this little, familiar face appeared. Ah! He was worried what had happened to me so decided to come back up! It was decided that I would go down backwards, like a baby! Half way down, Owen asked if I wanted a break. In no uncertain terms I replied, "No". All I could think about was Princess, Sam and a large glass of white wine! So, we kept going and boy, was I relieved and happy when we reached the bottom. And yes! I had a large glass of white wine.

We were around the pool at the resort and it began to rain quite heavily, so a crowd of us congregated around the thatched, roof bar. It was an all inclusive hotel so the drinks were flowing like water! It was such fun as there wasn't a lot of room and we were all huddled together laughing and having a great time. At 5.30 pm we decided to go and have a lay down and arranged to meet up at 7.30. No way! We didn't wake up until the following morning! Another good time had by all!

This holiday was two centred, so after a week we took a boat from Cancun to Cozumel, which is an island in the Caribbean Sea. Another couple from Scotland, who also had the same deal, were with us which was nice as we had just spent a week with them. On one of the days we all decided to hire a jeep and explore the island. It was wonderful and we stopped at a 'shack' and had the most delicious fajitas ever! We swam in the sea and found a shop where I bought an abundance of souvenirs! The evening entertainment was fabulous but one evening, sitting ready for it to begin, there was an announcement. It said that Michael Jackson had taken a detour to America to appear at our resort and would be arriving shortly! Not long after, a stretch limousine arrived and who out stepped out, Michael Jackson! Well, not really but he was a very good tribute act and the whole scenario was done extremely well.

Unfortunately, Princess went missing! She was very beautiful and we are convinced that she was stolen and sold!

Two stories come to mind whilst living in Sharbatley. Owen and I had been to friends for a social evening and as we walked home I spotted a bush that I decided would look really nice in our garden, so I asked Owen to relocate it! He had white trousers on but was up for the challenge! He began pulling on it and I got a huge fit of the giggles. The more Owen kept asking me to be quiet the worse I became. It was hilarious! We got the bush home and Owen planted it! The next day, we were a little apprehensive to see how the tree had been planted, but to our delight and amazement, it was perfectly upright and solid. Well-done Owen!

The second story involves our cat Sam. There had been quite a downfall of rain one evening and Sam was outside. The rain had flooded the path by about 4 inches. I called Sam and he appeared, trudging through the water like mummy's little soldier.

Sam loved climbing trees but he wasn't very clever at climbing back down! Owen wore a white shirt every day to the office and of course showered every morning. This particular morning, Sam had gone out and decided to climb the tree outside our bedroom window. He was obviously in trouble as we could hear him meowing! So, Owen, all showered and in his nice, white shirt went out, climbed the tree and carried mummy's little soldier down. Then, showered again and put on another white shirt!

Let me tell you about Sam and 'broast'. We could not eat a broast without him because he absolutely loved it! I would always have the spicy one and Owen would have the regular. We also bought a prawn one which came with a lovely Rose Marie sauce, which Sam and I shared. He could have devoured a whole one if permitted but it was also one of my favourites As soon as he had a whiff of it he would meow constantly, jump onto the coffee table and go crazy until it was within his grasp! Of course, it was far too hot to eat immediately so I found myself 'hahing' on it to feed his insatiable appetite! Owen would be leisurely enjoying his chicken and coleslaw because Sam also preferred my spicy chicken! His love for 'chilli was also extraordinary'! He would have his own bowl with rice and grated cheese on top and the three of us would eat together!

Another trip Owen and I took was to Florida, the south-eastern region of America. We visited all the expected attractions but wanted to do something different so decided to book a flight on 'Howard Hughes's' 4 seated airplane. It was the original plane he used to take his family on holiday to Mexico. It was phenomenal, if not a little bit scary. I was sat next to the pilot and he asked me if I wanted to fly it! Of course I said yes, even though I was a bit nervous. I knew that he would be supervising me but it was very exciting taking the wheel. Owen was so jealous, as I was actually flying the plane!

Owen loves lobster, so on a visit to a seafood restaurant Owen decided to order two! The waitress, very kindly suggested that he should only order one to begin with as they were 'Maine' lobsters and extremely large! Eventually, she convinced him so he only ordered one. When she brought it to the table it was enormous, overlapping the plate! Owen appeared a little embarrassed and thanked her for persuading him to only order one as no way could he have eaten two!

CHAPTER 20 THE HASH HOUSE HARRIERS

A friend of mine at the hospital was a member of 'The Hash House Harriers', a running group that went out into the desert every Thursday. She invited us to join her, so when Thursday came, armed with our water bottle and suitable attire (underneath my Abaya) we followed a trail of vehicles into the desert!

The Jeddah HHH's were called JH3 and were a very family, orientated group, where as in some countries; it is directed more towards adults.

OMG! Where do I begin? There were hundreds of people, different ages and nationalities who gathered at a designated spot which was called, 'the car park'. There were two runs. The 'main' was for the more 'active' or 'serious' runner (competitive) and the other was the family run, and also for the less active! (Me!) I very stupidly had opted to go on the main run which was pretty tough and the terrain was quite challenging under foot. I huffed and puffed, just to keep up, although I did manage to mutter to Owen that this was NOT the way I wanted to spend a Thursday and that I would NEVER EVER return! Well, that was not strictly true. Owen absolutely loved it and wanted to go again the week after and the week after, you get the picture? So, a trip into the desert became a weekly event. After the run, there was this traditional dance and 'chant!' which I will try and relive for you. Here we go! Firstly, we all formed a circle. Then, you would turn out your thumbs, bend your knees and start chanting. ; Shubida, shubida, shubida dah dah! shubida, shubida, shubida dah! As you chanted this little ditty, you had to change direction with your thumbs. Then, we would throw our hands in the air and sing, "we're singing in the rain, just singing in the rain, what a wonderful feeling, I'm happy again" whilst turning around! Owen taught my niece and nephew this ritual when they were kids. They loved it and did a special performance for their mum and dad.

The person (usually a man) in charge was called, 'The Grand Master', and the committee, were called 'The Polit Bureau'. Also serving on the committee was a hash 'scribe', who would take notes on each run/event and then produce a 'hash mag' that was given out the following week. There was also the 'RA' (religious advisor)' who would be responsible for giving out punishments to those that violated the rules of the 'hash'. The punishment was usually a 'gunging', which involved sitting the offender (s) on a chair and then dousing them with a large bucket full of cold, coloured water! There was also, 'hash cash', responsible for collecting money each week and paying expenses.

The runs were laid on the Friday morning of the previous week, with 'chalk'. The people who laid the 'trails' were called 'hares' and they were also responsible for the safety of the 'harriers (runners)' during the 'runs'. There was always a hare behind the last runner for support and who also acted as a safety net. It cost ten riyals (approx 2 pounds) to go on a 'hash' (run) to cover the cost of water and oranges for the 'orange stop'. On many occasions, after the run, a lot of people would stay out in the desert, have a bar-b-que and just 'chill!'

Everybody had a 'hash handle', which was a special name that reflected your personality. Mine was 'Falcon' because my family name is Peregrine. Owen's was 'warthog' for reasons we won't go into! There is one other person that Knows the reason, Angie, if you are reading this, do you remember? Lol.

When you had completed 25 runs you were rewarded with an engraved, pewter, beer mug. It was a very nice memento and a great reminder of the Hash. When multiples of 25 were completed, another one was awarded. The quality of the award improved the more runs you achieved. The same applied if you completed, 5 'hares'. Laying the trails was a big responsibility as they had to be suitable for the more serious runners and the families. Opting to be a hare also meant that you had to get up early on a Friday morning. Mind you, after making the effort to get up early, the temperature at that time of the morning was lovely and it was a great feeling to be up, driving into the desert.

Owen and I had a collection which we value as they remind us of what a fabulous time we had!

We both loved JH3 but I wasn't keen on doing my ablutions behind a rock, so I asked Owen to make me a portable toilet! He took it very seriously and went out and bought a 'toilet tent'. He then cut a hole out of the seat of a plastic chair where he inserted a large black bin liner. It worked very well but he wanted to improve it. The second model, 'mark 2' was a wooden box with a proper toilet seat on top and a plastic bag inside. Inside the tent we also put toilet rolls, air freshener, wet wipes and a lamp. It turned out that a lot of people didn't like 'pooing' behind a rock because it wasn't too long before other hashers would come and ask to use it, especially the ladies. It became so popular that there would be a queue! But, there was a downfall! The 'Polit bureau' decided that our 'toilet' was a 'gungable' offence because it was considered an unnecessary extra! So, we had cold, coloured water poured all over us in front of everyone! Hey, that's the way it was, good, clean fun!

There was an annual dinner held in various compounds as they all had function rooms. There was always a DJ within the community equipped with a great selection of music or a band that wanted to exercise their talents. Awards were given out for personal incidents that had happened throughout the year. For example, a friend of ours became rather 'silly' at one of the hashes, so was awarded 'plonker' of the year. It was a lot of fun and great seeing everybody in their 'glad rags'. Another friend, Mark, wanted to dress in something a little bit more 'flamboyant' so he and Owen had 'special' shirts made! They looked completely normal with their DJ's on but when they removed them, the back and sleeves were made from the most outrageous material that you could imagine. They went down a storm and became a regular dress code for future events. I bought a fabulous pair of gold, very high platform shoes which cost me 500 riyals (100 pounds)! That was the first and last time I ever spent that much money on a pair of shoes! And, I didn't fall over! The usual 'falling down water' was in abundance and a good time was had by all!

Owen would get so excited when Thursday came around. We were extremely lucky, because his company gave him a four wheel drive, which was far more efficient for driving across the desert terrain. When you came close to the part of road that you would turn off and go into the desert, there would be a 'convoy' of vehicles all looking for the great outdoors! It was at a different location every week so a map would be available to pick up informing you where the turn off was.

We would often stay over night when the temperature wasn't too intense and for the enthusiasts an early morning run at 7.00. Somebody would be responsible for bringing tea, coffee etc. and they were called 'hash nibbles'. A funny story comes to mind! On the morning after, Maggie, in charge of breakfast, filled the kettle with what she thought was water! Wrong! It was 'sid!' (Our homemade 'falling down' water!')

I didn't have the pleasure of drinking it but those that did, had an early morning buzz!

CHAPTER 21 A NEW CHALLENGE

I was still working at The King Fahd and had been given a promotion, which now meant that I was responsible for all the dental nurses, the schedules and the ordering of supplies. The job was very fulfilling and I was flattered that I had been chosen to take on the role. Inga, a colleague of mine had changed her job and had gone to work for the 'Female College of Health Sciences'. Her position was' Head of the Dental department'; teaching Saudi ladies how to become Dental Nurses, up to British standards. She asked if I would like to join her as a teacher as they needed more British staff. I gave the offer a great deal of thought and decided to accept! I was always looking to enhance my career and for new challenges so transferred and joined her at the college. The working hours were shorter, the salary was better and there were more holidays!

During one of the holidays of the college I decided to visit a health farm for two weeks. I chose one in St. George, Utah, Nevada, USA. It was quite exciting as the journey involved an overnight stay in Las Vegas! During my stay at the health farm, I booked a trip to 'Zion National Park'. The scenery was spectacular and 'breathtaking'! It was an awesome trip because from America, I went home for a week, unbeknown to my dad. My mum was very good at squeezing information out of me and would constantly ask when I was going home. So, in the end she got it out of me that I was coming home for my dad's birthday. Rick, my brother in law picked me up from Heathrow and took me to his and Helen's house where mum and dad were going that evening. I hid in their kitchen and at the appropriate moment, walked out with a beer for dad! He was absolutely 'gobsmacked' but very happy.

Another surprise visit comes to mind. Mum and dad were going to Majorca for a holiday and I decided to surprise them! I asked Helen to find out which hotel they were staying in and to book me in either the same one or one close by.

Whenever I asked Helen to help me arrange something, she was always very obliging and took it all in her stride. There were times when I asked her to do some very obscure things!

She managed to book me into a hotel nearby. I arrived at the hotel around mid-night but wanted to see if I could find my parents so took my suitcase to the hotel room, grabbed my room key some money and set off, much to the hotel's astonishment! I walked for about 5 minutes and well, I couldn't believe my eyes, saw them in a bar! I cautiously approached and slowly put my head behind the door, close to where they were sitting. They turned around and spotted me. Their faces were a 'picture' of delight and disbelief! My mum kept pinching me to see if I was real! We rang Helen the next day to let her know that I had arrived.

The college worked in conjunction with Glasgow health authority so the Nursing director was from Glasgow. A lot of the other staff were Scottish but there were also, Irish and Lebanese. A simulated surgery, equipped with a fully operational chair and instruments had been installed. This of course was an invaluable asset for the practical side of the course. The head of department left and I was asked to step in! A completely new challenge for me and sometimes very frustrating as a Saudi member of my team just didn't want to conform! I think it's called 'arrogant!'

A lady examiner came from the UK to test the students on the practical side and also brought with her the theory papers which were sent back to the UK to be marked.

An incident comes to mind that occurred in the garden of the college. It was a lovely day and a perfect temperature, so I suggested to the students that we take the lesson outside. A nice idea you would think? The ladies removed their head scarves as there were no male students! But, as we were in the midst of the lesson, a Pilipino, male workman appeared and walked in front of them! OMG! The reaction from the ladies was unbelievable! They tried to hide under their chairs whilst scrambling for their scarves! The expression on their faces and the screaming was intense! It was actually frightening and very embarrassing. I genuinely felt very sorry for them so from then onwards, the workmen were informed if lessons were to be conducted outside.

I became very friendly with four other teachers and we would invite them over at weekends. They lived in housing provided by the college so their social life was very limited as male visitors would not have been permitted.

We would have a blast and quote, 'dance our toe nails off!' until 4 in the morning!

Owen's boss Mike lived in a compound called 'Mura Bustan', so we would often visit him on a Friday when I would cook him a roast chicken dinner. On one occasion he was watching a 'James Bond' film in French! Owen, a bit confused said," I didn't know you spoke French Mike?" Mike replied, "I don't", Mike replied, "but I've seen it so many times, I know what they're saying"!

Another extremely funny scenario that occurred with Mike happened in his office. First of all, let me explain that British newspapers were available, but they arrived a few days later in the supermarkets than dated, because they had to be vetted for any contraband that may offend Muslims e.g. skimpily dressed ladies, so Mike asked the 'tea boy', (who didn't speak a lot of English) to go and buy him 'The Mail on Sunday'. The tea boy looked very confused as it was Thursday and said, "Mr Mike, today it Thursday, I get it for you on Sunday!" Mike was becoming more and more agitated, (he wasn't the most patient of people) and frustratingly said, "I know it's not Sunday, the paper doesn't get here until Thursday"! This went on for a while but eventually, the tea boy caught on.

It was the 31st of August 1997 and most of you will know what I'm about to say. Yes, the day Princess Diana died. I was in the shower, getting ready for work at 6 a.m. and Owen came rushing in to say that Princess Diana and Dodi Fayed had been involved in a car crash, in Paris. I was devastated as I found her a breath of fresh air. Then it was announced that they had been killed, along with their driver, Henri Paul. The funeral was going to take place during work hours so a few of us asked if we could watch it in work, as the western teachers lived on the college grounds and had satellite television. The Principal very kindly agreed so we all sat together to watch the very sad and momentous occasion.

CHAPTER 22 PINK FLAMINGO

In1997, after 6 years in Sharbatly, a Turkish friend of ours found a very nice, small compound with 10, three storey villas, a pool and a recreation centre. It was 'pink' so called 'Flamingo! All the villas were empty and he wanted to fill it with ex-pats. Owen's company paid for his housing and it was cheaper than Sharbatly so we couldn't let this opportunity pass us by. We agreed to take one and chose the one that looked down the whole of the compound. The villas surrounded the pool, so basically, you stepped out of your back door, onto your balcony and the pool was just a few steps away. It was fabulous! The compound was brand new so we had 'carte blanch' on the décor and furnishings. Owen's company were very generous and gave him a sum of money to help furnish it. It was an incredible experience shopping in Jeddah as the shops were open until very late at night and anything you purchased was generally delivered the same day. So, at 10.a.m.one morning we went and chose carpet for our bedroom. The fitter followed us home, measured the room, returned to the shop, cut the carpet to size and then returned to fit it! OMG! In the afternoon, we went and chose a bedroom suite which was also delivered the same day at 5p.m. On the ground floor we had a dining room, lounge, a huge kitchen and a guest toilet. The lounge opened up onto the balcony which over looked the pool. We purchased a leather suite and had scatter rugs on the marble floor. In the dining room we bought a wicker table with a glass top and six matching chairs. There was a beautiful long and winding staircase leading up to the first floor. We decorated the wall with framed programmes showcasing all the productions we'd been in. During a trip to one of the 'souks' we bought some Saudi instruments which were also mounted on the wall. The first floor is where we had our TV room, three bedrooms (one ensuite) and another full bathroom. There was also a kitchenette equipped with a small fridge to keep drinks in, Sam's food and a microwave.

Sam would only eat cat food if it had tuna fish in water mixed with it! If it was taken from the fridge it had to go in the microwave for 20 seconds because he wouldn't eat it cold! We asked our friend Stewart to come and 'Sam sit' whilst we took a short vacation. Stewart became worried that Sam wasn't eating enough, so he visited some friends living on the compound to ask their advice. Sarah immediately said," Do you stand with him"? Stewart was bewildered and said, "What"! So Sarah replied, "You have to stand with him when he's eating otherwise he won't eat"! Stewart was amused but at Sam's next meal he stood with him and he ate every little bit. Mind you, he looks up at you regularly to make sure that you are still standing there.

On the 24th of June 1998, Owen and I got married in Jeddah! Yes! We were legally married at the British Consulate by the Consul General, Innes Ray. He showed us a document that gave him permission from The Queen, that he could legally marry us. It was a lovely day as close friends, Viv and Ali were witnesses and we were offered a 'proper' drink as the consulate is considered to be on British ground. We had the reception on our compound, which was catered by The '

Movenpick' Hotel. It was a memorable day which was made perfect with Sam, wearing a tartan 'Dickie bow'. A Saudi colleague of Owen's unexpectedly brought a belly dancer to the reception which was very entertaining and of course extremely unique. She was stunning and bewitched our guests with her tantalizing moves. Our wedding invitation was a 'one off' as it resembled a theatre programme, naming the show as 'The Wedding', featuring, Jane and Owen in the leading roles and friends as the extra's! We were given some lovely gifts but I have to say that our favourite one was a 5ft, wrought iron candelabrum which will always be on display.

So, when you get married, one has to have a special pair of shoes! There is a street in Jeddah called 'Sary' Street which has an abundance of shoe shops. In the first shop I found a very nice pair of gold, kitten heeled ones with an ankle strap. They also had some hand stitching around the toe which really finished them off. I really liked them but it was only the first shop so we went up and down this very, long street and guess what? Went back and bought the first pair! I had no idea how much they were but I didn't really care. They were for my wedding day! When I asked the price, I thought my hearing had been impaired as the assistant said 50 riyals! "50 riyals", I said" so he then said, "Ok, 45"! That was only nine pounds! So of course I said, "Yes"! But I gave him the 50. I still have them in the original box.

The real down fall was that none of our families were able to attend our wedding but that was rectified in August when we went back to Somerset and had a blessing for family and friends in the chapel where my parents were married. Owen and Rick wore kilts and I had a dress made with a handkerchief bottom We tried to get Jacob, who was 8 at the time to wear a kilt, but there was no way on this Earth that he was going to wear a 'skirt'! We had a lovely reception at a local hotel called, 'The Tudor', which was owned by a friend. Another friend played her key board and my nephew Jacob, played his guitar and Hannah, then 12, played her oboe. My dad's brother and sister came over from Wales which was extra special. Mike, the owner of the hotel, put us in the wedding suite as a gift which had a four poster bed. It was very generous of him and we had a glorious day.

As we were home we decided to book a honeymoon. We decided on 'The Dominican Republic', in the Caribbean. It was a long journey from Gatwick airport but well worth the journey because when we arrived it was a beautiful resort and the temperature of the pool was perfect. We decided to take a trip to see a bit of the area and how better than on a horse! The lady who owned the stables was German and seemed delighted that she had contact with other westerners. We mounted our horses and 'set off' but they knew exactly where they were going. It started to rain heavily but we were able to find shelter in a barn. When it stopped raining we continued our trek which took us to a 'rickety', run down bar. There were chickens roaming around in the straw on the floor. We were handed a bottle of coke but it had a strange taste, Bacardi had been added, unbeknown to us! There were a group of Dominican men sitting at a table drinking a bottle of 'Johnny Walker', a whiskey very close to Owen's heart, so he went over and gestured that he was Scottish and would like to help them drink their whiskey! They were very obliging and asked him to join them. I must say that he only had one, just to be friendly. By the time we got back to the hotel we were pretty 'sqiffy' but decided to go to the bar and have a few more little 'tipples'. Another early night!

We returned to Jeddah and resumed our extraordinary lives.

We also had a unique wedding ceremony on the 'hash'! The Grand Master and his wife had become good friends and to our surprise, organised a 'wedding, hash style!' I was wrapped in a white curtain and Owen was given top hat and waistcoat. We looked like 'the bees knees'. The GM had constructed a 'dog collar' and written wedding vows that would never be used in a church ceremony! They were very cleverly written and promises made that Owen would pay my credit card bills at all times and that I would be respectful and cater to his every needs! They had also organised a cake and of course, all the other hashers were the congregation. A fantastic time was had by one and all and another memorable occasion.

A friend of mine performed as a 'clown' for children's parties and asked if I'd be interested as she was short staffed. It sounded fun so she fixed me up with a very colourful clown's outfit and taught me 'the ropes'. I had a fabulous pair of handmade desert boots that I'd bought in Glastonbury. They were multi-coloured with palm trees painted on them! My dad was with me when I bought them and he had a very funny sense of humour, so when I finally chose a pair, my dad piped up and said, "It's my turn now!" The look on the sales assistant's face was a picture, until she realized that he was joking then burst into laughter! It was very funny!

My violin was at home and I wanted to bring it to Jeddah, now that I was playing in JLO. Owen was going back to the UK for business so we arranged that my brother in law would drive up to Heathrow with it, meet up with Owen and hand it over. Pretty straight forward you might say but it didn't happen! Owen was waiting in Terminal 4 and Rick was in Terminal 3! I had misinformed Rick which terminal to go to, so I didn't get my violin that trip.

We had a lovely Indian man Mohammad who looked after the compound. In Saudi, he is called the 'Harris'. We all looked after him and gave him gifts to celebrate the end of 'Ramadan'. He did a lot of walking to purchase different items so our friend John decided to buy him a bike! Oh dear, Mohammad was not happy. He came to us and quote," Why Mr John buy me bike? I no need for bike." He was almost in tears. I think he really wanted the money as he was having a house built in India and his wife was expecting. So, we told John. He took it very well, sold the bike and gave the money to Mohammad. Everyone was happy!

To celebrate the millennium a group of us decided to rent some villas at a compound out near the beach which was used by Saudi Airline staff. It was quite luxurious and there was a pool to every villa. We shared with a couple, Mike and Theresa who were also members of the beach cabin. We had also rented a function room where everybody gathered for the evening. Just before midnight we all went outside because there was a firework display that was absolutely spectacular! At 3 a.m., midnight in the U.K. someone had organised a 'piper', Ron Beatson. He was outstanding and it was especially patriotic for Owen. The next morning we related to Mike and Theresa that we had stayed up late to watch the firework celebrations around the world. Theresa quite seriously said,"Oh, could you see them from here"? Owen and I just collapsed into laughter and thankfully Mike also saw the funny side of it as well. We became very good friends with Ron and his wife Yolly and often went to his villa which he had named,' The Scottish Consulate'! Gosh! We had some fun nights there as Ron was able to get hold of the real Mcoy!

Owen was 50 in August 2000 and I wanted to buy him something special! A Rolls Royce! Owen had a passion for them and a second hand one isn't as expensive as you would imagine. Once again, I solicited help from my sister, Helen. I'll never forget the phone call I made to her asking her to find me one, she just said, "Okay"! The landlord and landlady of the local pub at home (The Cottage) were from London and had a lot of contacts with classic cars, in fact Gerry drove a Bentley so Helen asked them to help her find one. They were delighted and contacted their friends in London. Helen would ring me in Saudi and advise me on what was available. I obviously had to make sure that Owen didn't hear the phone calls and catch on. I settled on a '1978 peacock blue Silver Shadow'. The owner of the show room in London drove it to

Bridgwater, where it was taken to the garage in the village under hiding. I asked Barry (owner of the village garage) to put some balloons on it and an air freshener inside but he point blank refused, stating that you don't hang balloons on a Rolls Royce or cover up the smell of the leather interior! That told me!

So we travelled home and stayed with my dad. On the day of Owen's birthday I had arranged Barry to drive it up at 10a.m. I was so excited and of course my dad was in the picture. I kept looking out the window and then it arrived! All the neighbours came out to see it. It was a beautiful example of the 'marque! I called Owen and asked him to look out of the window. I can't explain the look on his face. He was speechless and flabbergasted! We took my dad out for a run and you could see he felt like a king. We stayed overnight in a hotel and were looking out of our hotel room window, which overlooked the car park. There was an elderly couple standing next to it having their picture taken. They were beaming with delight! We also drove it up to the Highlands of Scotland. We kept it for 2 years and rented a barn to house it in which wasn't really suitable. Also, it wasn't being driven so electrical and mechanical parts were beginning to fail. Our friend Stewart bought it which kind of kept it in the family.

We hosted a number of events on the compound and one was 'Horse racing '. A large screen is put up and the pre recorded races are run after you choose a numbered horse and place your bet. They're great fun because the ladies wear hats like at 'Ascot'! On one particular evening our friend Jon decided to dress up as 'The Queen'! He looked fabulous with long white gloves, sash, a crown and of course a very regal 'wave'.

David, another good friend of ours was approaching his 50th birthday and somehow acquired a whole 'pig' which we housed in our chest freezer. He hired two Filipino men to spit roast it up on the roof! It took six hours to cook and you could smell it all over the compound! David wanted to spend the Thursday evening at the beach so we all obliged and greedily ate the 'spit-roasted pork' It was absolutely delicious! David saved a leg which we had the next day in our house with left over fried–up jacket potatoes, veg and gravy. Another gastronomic delight!

Another memorable evening was an evening of entertainment at the beach. Owen and David performed a skit of 'The Two Ronnie's' and a few of the girls danced 'The Can Can' where they were given a standing ovation. Their routine was extremely energetic and they dressed appropriately with fish nets and feathers!

A new stage was built at Jeddah Prep for the 'Music Man', by Meredith Willson. Our friend, Ron Beatson,(who was a senior manager of Pepsi Cola), arranged for Pepsi to sponsor the building of a new stage. That's another story, because during a performance, the stage began to collapse and I, who was in the middle of a marching dance routine saw the conundrum and somehow managed to divert the rest of the dancers around it! Wow! That could have been such a disaster on so many levels.

During a vacation home Owen and I took my dad on a trip back to Wales to visit one of his brother's families. Dad wasn't able to drive now due to ill health but kept his car for Helen and me to drive. It was only a two hour drive over 'The Severn Bridge', an easy journey to do in a day. We arranged to meet my Uncle, Auntie and cousin in a restaurant for lunch. Afterwards, we were going to my cousin Linda's for a cup of tea. As we left the restaurant, Linda suggested I follow her car, which was red! A good plan you would think! But, unbeknown to me, I was following the wrong car! It stopped in front of a house who I assumed was Linda's! We helped dad out of the car with each of us both sides of him and proceeded to walk down the drive. A man was tending the garden, who I assumed was the gardener and a lady who I didn't recognise came out of the house, who I thought was a friend of my cousins. The lady eventually asked if we needed any help, so I replied, "its ok, we can manage". We carried on walking when she said again, in a very irritated manner, "but where are you going"? "My cousin lives here", I replied and once again, in an even more irritated voice said, "Who's your cousin"? You can guess the rest! My dad was becoming a bit irritated so we carefully turned him round and went back to the car where I rang my cousin! Oh, it doesn't stop there! When we eventually reached Linda's house I thought her son was her husband and on the way back to Somerset I went into the wrong lane and we nearly ended up in Birmingham! My Aunty rang dad's house in the evening to check that we had reached home. What a good laugh we had! I was relating this story to my sister who related it to some friends in the local swimming pool. Apparently they were in hysterics and the whole pool erupted into screams of laughter. You don't know my sister but you should know that she has an infectious, huge laugh and has no inhibitions about hiding it! .

A very funny story comes to mind one evening at the beach cabin. Our friend Ron plays the bagpipes and brought them to the beach to play as the sun went down. So, after a great day relaxing on the beach and swimming in the sea, we all showered, sat on the veranda with a refreshing drink and looked forward to the entertainment. Ron headed down onto the beach with his pipes but on the way, Owen stopped him and suggested they have a bit of fun! Owen had found a broken beach chair and for some reason turned it upside down. The four legs resembled 'pipes'! Everybody was engaged in their own little 'chit chat' so didn't notice what was going on, apart from me and my friend Trish. Ron hid underneath the cabin with his bagpipes and Owen walked down onto the beach. They began playing' the bagpipes and 'chair 'in sync'. Well, this particular guy, who was a little under the influence said," He's very good, isn't he?"! My friend Trish and I 'lost it' and almost 'peed' our pants.

Bill Scot, (Scottish dentist,) asked if I could supply him with two nurses that would be suitable to work in his practice. Gosh, what a responsibility! I really wanted to get this right and not let him down. I decided to ask two Saudi girls that I had worked with previously at the 'King Fahd'. They had spent time out of Saudi and I had found them reliable and responsible. They were also very good friends and spoke excellent English.

Part of my job at the college was to place students into outside clinics so that they could experience working with dentists and patients in real life situations. I had two students at the King Fahd so would return regularly to offer support and assess their progress. I was also able to rekindle friendships with old colleagues. I approached the two girls that I had decided on and asked if they would be interested in my proposal. They seemed very interested so I discussed the job description with them and made it clear that I didn't want Mr. Scot let down. I think they were flattered that I had chosen them and agreed to meet him and discuss the details. I'm pleased to say that it all worked out very well. Bill was very happy and impressed and they stayed with him until he retired a few years later.

I decided to leave the college as Glasgow Health Authority lost the contract and it was taken over by the Saudi Ministry of Education. The running of the college changed and my friends and I became disillusioned, to say the least! Most of them left and I wasn't able to function and continue as before due to the changes.

CHAPTER 23 TIME FOR ANOTHER CAREER CHANGE AND GET RE-EDUCATED!

A friend informed me that 'The Bangladeshi International School' was looking for native, English speaking people to teach at the School, so I applied. The principal was British and she suggested that I teach a grade 1 class (5 year olds) to see how I got on. There was a lot of support and a curriculum to follow so I accepted and became a first grade teacher.

The kids were from a variety of countries and their parents were very grateful and exceptionally keen for their children to excel. In fact, they weren't happy if their grades slipped. I absolutely loved teaching and the kids so decided to take it further and have a change of career!

I had often thought about a change of career and remembered a conversation I had had with a lovely Irish dentist when working at the King Fahd. I mentioned that I would like a change and fancied the idea of teaching English. It would be another string to my bow (no pun intended!) living in the Middle East. He told me about a one month course called, C.E.L.T.A. (Certificate of English Language Teaching of Adults).

I decided to pursue this idea and wrote to 'International House' in London. They invited me for an interview, which I attended on a trip home in March, 2000 and was offered a place.

The course was in July. I opted to stay with a lady who provided bed, breakfast and evening meal. She was also C.E.L.T.A. accredited which was an asset as she would often help me if I had a problem.

I found the course extremely challenging but thankfully, the hard work paid off and I passed!

My sister managed to get hold of two Tina Turner tickets one weekend when I was in London, so she came up from Somerset and I booked us into a hotel for the night. Tina was performing at Wembley Stadium where she gave an unforgettable performance.

I returned to my job at the Bangladeshi school and resumed teaching my little darlings!

We had a big window in our living room upstairs and Sam used to love looking out of it. He would stand on the arm of the sofa and put his front paws on the window sill to look out so we decided to get him a shelf. We bought a pine one and he loved it! He would lay on it whenever we spent time upstairs and watch the world go by. We decided to redecorate the upstairs living room and painted Sam's shelf orange! OMG, he hated it and would not go on it! He would look at us as if to say, "What have you done to my shelf"? He would jump on it and realize that it wasn't the same. We think that it was the smell of the paint that put him off. Anyway, poor Sam missed his shelf so much that we went out and bought him another one!

It was a rarity that we would put Sam in a 'cattery' when we took a vacation. I didn't like the thought of him being somewhere unfamiliar but luckily, we had an abundance of friends that were willing to come and stay in our house and 'cat sit'. We would make sure that they were well catered for as far as food and drink was concerned because it was comforting to know that he was well looked after. Mind you, our friends thought it a huge responsibility and confessed that they were glad to see us return. They found it 'nerve racking', in case he went missing or got hurt. He always knew when we were going away when the 'suitcases' appeared. We had to close the bedroom door otherwise he would 'pee' in them to voice his disapproval! On our return he would ignore us by sitting like a 'chicken' with his bottom facing us. It was really funny; it was as if he was saying, "So you're home then"! Although, it didn't take him long before he would to jump up and be loved!

There were times when we had to make other arrangements for him so I asked around and an American couple, Edna and Ernie were recommended. I rang them and they invited me to come and take a look at their home, to put my mind at rest. They were extremely nice and understood my concerns. He wasn't going to be confined to one room but had to share with some dogs behind a child friendly gate! That didn't bother Sam. He would annoy the dogs by jumping over the fence and if they irritated him, he would smack them on their nose with his paw. We were very happy to leave him there and he became quite a celebrity! When we collected him Earnie had something to show us. He had to mount his computer keyboard high up on the wall because Sam would lay right across it and prevent Ernie from working! Earnie and Edna became good friends and moved onto our compound which was a bonus when we went on vacation.

On a trip back to Jeddah we had an overnight stay in London and took a trip into 'Covent Garden'. During one trip we sat and had caricatures drawn which we hung in the guest toilet. They were extremely funny and certainly a talking point. Perusing round the market I spotted these collectable, limited edition handmade dolls, about 2ft tall. The one that caught my eye was a 'hobo' clown dressed in brown, turned up corduroy trousers, a brown contrasting flannelette cloak, a mustard waist coat, flat cap and big, bulbous shoes, playing his violin. He was called 'Ziggy' and I just had to have him. He was boxed up and came back to Jeddah with us.

On one of the religious holidays Owen suggested we went to Bali. We loved it there even though it was fairly quiet due to the 'Bali bombings! It was preferable to hire a driver to take you sightseeing because you could go and stop where ever you wanted plus, they were very reasonable. We hired a young man called Wayang, and asked him to take us to a furniture factory. Oh dear! We came away with 2 teak empire four poster beds, an extremely large table with eight chairs, a bar, a corner unit, a dresser, a carvery, two coffee tables, two stools and a variety of 'Lombok' pots and pottery! Everything was so cheap, as well as being unique, beautifully carved and decorated.

It arrived in Jeddah 3 weeks after in a 40 ft container! It took 4 men to lift out the table top out and 2 hours to fully empty it! Our villa looked amazing and we couldn't wait to have a party and show it off!

A very good friend of ours, Jon, was extremely talented at interior decorating, so we asked him if he had any ideas about drapes. We also wanted him to decorate one of the four poster beds that was in our room. He took us down to the 'Indian' souk (market) and we bought a mixture of coloured 'sari's', along with gold and burnt orange voile. He dressed the dining room windows with the burnt orange voile. They looked spectacular! He also dressed our four poster bed with gold voile across the top which looked like a sea of shimmering beauty and the sari's draped down giving the effect of a 'boudoir', where all your fantasies could come true! It was a show stopper!

The dining table, also made from teak was unique! It had knot holes in it and the wood was 'distressed' to give the allusion of authenticity. Owen loved to tell tales, in fact, they just rolled off his tongue, particularly if he found a gullible person. One such person was a very good friend, Clem. At a gathering, Clem made a comment about the table. Owen launched into a story that it had been salvaged from a 'Pirate ship' that plied its trade through the Straits of Malacca! Clem was taken in, 'Hook, line and sinker!' Clem related this story to a friend of his who happened to be the headmaster of the British school (his wife Trish taught there). He then invited Owen to come and give a talk to some of the pupils at the school! Oh dear! All had to be revealed, but boy, did we have a good laugh over it!

Whilst in Bali we decided to go on the 'Hash'. Two friends were also with us, Trevor and Edna. We found out where the 'car park' was and arranged a taxi to take us there. There were a lot of ex-pats at the site and a lot of beer! After every one had partaken in refreshments, we set off. There was only a main run and I found it hard to keep up so Owen walked with me. There was also a Canadian man who found it difficult so he joined us. The terrain was very different from Jeddah and the trail wasn't laid with chalk but rice. We lost the trail and ended up going through 'rice paddies'. It began to get dark and we were getting a bit worried so I suggested that we try and 'flag' a vehicle down to take us to the police station. Luckily, some young men stopped in a van and complied with our request. The nearest town was called 'Tampaxearring' and the police officer appeared rather amused when we related our story to him but also very helpful and arranged a taxi to take us back to our hotel. Trevor and Edna had gone back to the hotel when the hash was over. We didn't leave our hotel room that night as we were exhausted and my legs were sore, so I had a hot bath, ordered club sandwiches, copious quantities of alcohol and watched the film 'Red Dragon'. Edna was extremely relieved when we spoke to her later on but Trevor hadn't been too concerned on the assumption that Owen was a sensible chap! I think we were very lucky as anything could have happened!

We loved Bali so much that we decided to spend another vacation there. Owen was keen to go on the Bali Hash again but I decided to stay in the 'car park', safe and sound! We found out where the car park was it was and organised a taxi. The taxi driver went and sat with the other drivers and waited for us. I couldn't see him from where I was sitting and didn't realise that he was 'drinking' alcohol! On the return journey, we realized that his driving was very erratic! He was drunk! I was quite frightened because it was dark and I had to keep asking him to slow down! We arrived back at the hotel in one piece but I refused to pay him!

Oliver! Oliver! Yes, another successful production put on by JLO at 'Jeddah Prep'. I played Mrs Bumble, a feisty character and Owen helped back stage with scenery changes and props. I had to sing with Mr Bumble, played by our friend Jon. (who dressed our house) He was trying to woo me so at the end of the song he pushed his head in between my breasts! Another audience pleaser!

I would sometimes bring home books to mark from school and spread them out on the dining room table. Sam decided that he didn't want mummy to do any marking and proceeded to sprawl all over them! Owen was upstairs watching T.V. so I would call up and ask him to call Sam. It worked for a while but then down he'd come and the process was repeated! What a boo-boo! He went missing for two days. We were beside ourselves and went out searching the immediate vicinity but to no avail! Oh dear, where was he? We were in bed but I woke up convinced that I'd heard a meow! It was 4 o clock but I didn't care. I rushed downstairs and opened the front door and in he ran like a bat out of hell! He was back! We think he got locked in a property that was being renovated and when the builders returned to work he ran out.

Another story comes to mind. My sister Helen and her husband Rick came out to Jeddah as Owen's company agreed to sponsor their visa. On a tour round the city we passed a roundabout of a giant thistle! I launched into this story that it had been presented to the city of Jeddah from the Lord Mayor of Edinburgh! Owen, all of a sudden said, "What?" I couldn't believe what he had said and suddenly realized that it was another 'porky' which I had fallen for, months ago! We took them out on the 'hash' but they found it too hot so the following week we took them up to Ta'if where the temperature was cooler and the air fresher. Helen came to school with me one day and taught a class of P.E. The kids responded very well and enjoyed it immensely. We also took them to the beach cabin which they loved.

We wanted to take Helen and Rick out for a nice meal and we knew exactly where to take them. There were a lot of excellent restaurants in Jeddah and one in particular was called 'Green Island'. It was set in glass pods which were situated in the 'Red Sea'. To reach the pods you had to walk on a walkway that was built on stilts. You could see 'schools' of fish from the walkway. It was quite a delightful experience and Helen and Rick had a memorable experience!

We went back to 'Green Island 'with our friend Stewart. He was able to arrange visa's to bring his sister and brother in law to Jeddah and one evening, unbeknown to them and me, had arranged a 'stretch limousine' to pick us all up from our house and take us to 'Green Island'. This vehicle was incredible! We got in and were taken on a tour of the city. We felt like royalty. The limousine returned to take us home, another unforgettable experience!

Another holiday comes to mind! We took a cruise on the river Nile but firstly had to fly to Cairo and stay overnight. The next morning we flew to Luxor where we boarded the boat. It wasn't the most 'grand' of boats and the cabin was dingy and claustrophobic but we decided to make the most of it. After all, we didn't have much choice! We headed up to the lounge area and ordered a drink. A couple were sitting there and we got chatting. Trevor was from Australia and his wife Florence was from Samoa. We instantly gelled and became good friends. Later on, Trevor was transferred from Riyadh and rented a house on our compound. We also made friends with an up and coming South African singer and his manager. In the evening we persuaded the manager of the night club to let him sing! We already knew a few people on the boat from Jeddah so we literally took over! Boy! We partied hard and long into the early hours, which seemed a good idea at the time but not at 4 a.m. when we had to get up and go on a sightseeing trip to the 'Valley of the Kings'. The trip organiser wanted to go to the sight early to avoid crowds and the hot sun. We were 'hanging' and couldn't wait to board the coach back. I promptly fell asleep and apparently began snoring. What happened next could have been grounds for divorce, according to other ladies on the coach. Owen asked the tour guide for the microphone and placed it in front of my face! So, the whole of the coach heard my dulcet tones! I woke up to rounds of applause and outbursts of laughter!

The boat cruised to Aswan where we disembarked and went shopping. It was horrendous because if you showed any interest in an item, the trader would hound you until you purchased it. They would even chase you down the road! I have to say that it spoilt the trip a bit.

The traditional sailboat of Egypt's river Nile is the 'Felucca'. Egyptians and foreigners can enjoy a relaxing ride, catching the breeze on a hot day or night. Owen, me and our friend Trevor decided to partake in a sail, so hired one. Trevor convinced the owner that he was able to sail it himself so we boarded this little boat and left the sailing in Trevor's capable hands! No! He had no idea how to steer it! We kept going around in circles and eventually, crashed into the pier, much to the owner's disgust! Luckily, there wasn't any harm done to the boat or us!

JH3 would represent all kinds of events and we became more and more involved, especially when a new GM was elected due to Paul's departure. So, a few of us decided to form a group called, the 'Goon squad' and be responsible for organising any social events. The 'Back to school' hash in September involved all kinds of live activities. To mention a few, hashers would stand behind a screen showing their bare feet and the team members would have to guess who they belonged too. We would concoct different drinks with all kinds of ingredients which the teams had to guess and David, had life size 'Jenga' wooden blocks made so teams would compete against each other. Simon, the music teacher from 'Conti' school came out with his keyboard and accompanied Owen and I, who attempted to sing a song from 'Phantom of the Opera'. A spotlight was shone on Owen on his entrance. It was electric! Everybody made an effort to dress up either as school kids or teachers wearing gowns and 'mortarboards'. OMG! We decided that it would be good fun to have teams 'line dance' so Sue and Keith gave a demonstration, as they belonged to a line dancing group. We wanted to set the GM up so we asked a friend of ours, Ron to help us. After a few of the teams had competed Ron stood up and said, "hey, it's all very well the Goon squad laughing and making fun of the novices, let's see if they can do it any better! Well, now it was our turn to shine! We played it very cool and said, "Okay, we'll have a go. Well, we rocked it with our cowboy hats and attitude because of course, we had been secretly practicing! Ian, the GM was blown away! We would pre-cook and transport all kinds of food into the desert using 'ban Maris', as well as organising bar-b-ques and seating made up of Arabic carpets and cushions.

I used to go home most of the school holidays to spend time with my dad. During one trip Owen decided to decorate the lounge! As I entered the house on my return I thought the sun was shining! He had painted the lounge bright yellow and orange! I couldn't believe my eyes! It was an abominable! I was speechless for a minute and then asked him if he was on drugs! He told me that Mohammad, the 'Harris' had seen it and said, "Mr Owen, it looks like curry house. I don't think Miss Jane will like" How right he was! I insisted on having it re-painted a very modest 'beige'.

Trevor and Florence joined JH3 when they moved into 'flamingo'. They had a very cute 'Pekinese 'dog called Coco who came with them on the 'hash '.But, he would get tired and Trevor would end up carrying him. So, his 'hash handle' was 'six pack'. He loved Sam and would follow him around the compound but Sam hated him! Sam would turn around and swipe him with his paw. Not very neighbourly!

Back to the 'hash'! Another memorable hash was 'bonfire night'. The first one we attended was incredible! There were hundreds of people and somebody had arranged an ice cream van to come out! The bonfire was colossal. Truck loads of wood were brought out to construct this piece of art which stood grand and erect and when it was lite, illuminated the sky. Somebody was able to get their hands on some 'fireworks which was the 'icing on the cake'.

CHAPTER 24 ROUNDABOUTS

The 'roundabouts' in Jeddah are unique, so I would like to tell you about some of the most magnificent ones. Jeddah is also home to some of the most creative sculptures that each has their own inspirational story.

'The Flying Car Magic Carpet' has a car on top of the carpet. It is designed using concrete and mosaic and highlights the theme of transport.

'The Camel' is in three parts; the front, the hump and the back.

'Al Falak Cosmos' sculpture was created by German artist Ottmar Hollman. It stands at 44 metres high and took 7 years to complete. It is one of the largest pieces of Art.

'The Lente' (lantern) has four pieces created from steel, ceramic and concrete. 'The Globe'part was built in the 1970's and stands on a surface of 600 metres.

'The Bicycle' was erected in 1982 and is made from white granite and black stone.

'The Verse Boat' roundabout was created by Julio Lafuente. It was inspired by the calligraphic sculpture 'Verse'.

'The knowledge' sculpture was built at the end of the 1950' and was created by Victor Vasarley. Its design incorporates trapezoids, diamonds and ovals. It implicates the vigorous and enterprising spirit.

'The Holy Koran' sculpture was built in the 1970's and created by Julio Lafluente. It was dedicated for the purpose of celebrating local culture and is adorned with calligraphic inscriptions and motifs.

'The Heart' sculpture was created by Saleh Abdulkarim and incorporates the use of marble. Saleh Abdulkarim was inspired by Mohamad Farsi who underwent open heart surgery in the 1980's, which is why it has a human form theme.

'The 20 flags of Victory' sculpture was made from scrap metal that came from rusted condensers. It implicates the victory flags that were used when conquering armies from Arab history.

'Al-qiblah' sculpture was designed by Julio Lafuente. It highlights local culture and is known by the name of 'Nike of Samothrace'. It took 5 years to complete and is set with 200 marbles and cement.

'Al-saroukh' was created by Francois Kovacs, who was influenced by his career in medicine. It is made from bronze and is 110cm high.

Our cat Sam was such a character. He had a particular party piece that we never tired of. When we had friends round, Owen would usually sit on the camel stool, much to Sam's annoyance, as it was his seat! So, to get his revenge, Sam would go to the door and ask to go out. Owen would of course oblige, get up from the stool and go to the door to let him out. Sam's plan always worked, as when he reached the door he would about turn and sit on the camel stool! You could almost hear him say, "Silly daddy!" Another adorable thing, Owen would pick him up and sit him in the corner of the settee like a teddy bear. He was just this black, fluffy mass of loveliness!

The most spectacular hash was at Christmas. The first one will always stick in my mind as it was unique and there had never been anything done like it before. Our friend David had access to a trailer which he thought could be turned into a sleigh. He also had a four wheel drive with a tow bar attached. I talked to the Art teacher at school and she agreed to come to 'Flamingo' and paint two pieces of identical wood that resembled the sides of a sleigh, which were then attached to the trailer. What a great job she did! David, John and Owen sawed out the scenes and attached them to the side of the trailer. I provided sausage rolls, mince pies and Christmas music to set the scene and of course we had our 'homemade' white 'grape juice' to help the festivities along! We were up until 2 a.m.! It was a complete secret to the rest of the 'Polit Bureau' so we were very excited for Thursday to come. So, on the Thursday, David attached the trailer/sleigh to his four wheel drive and we all set off for the designated spot. We left earlier to set everything up plus, we didn't want anybody else to see the sleigh. There were also a lot more festive goodies to set up, a tree, lights and Santa's grotto! An American friend of ours, Ernie agreed to be Santa and I, who had been 'Fairy Litharge' in the Christmas pantomime, was going to sit in the sleigh with him.

David drove the sleigh to the top of a hill so that nobody would see it. Ernie and I got into the sleigh and sat on two 'thrones' which David had fitted. (They were taken from one of the theatre containers, which was full of all genres of props). Back at the ranch, at the bottom of the hill, the rest of the goon squad began to psyche up the kids, asking them if they could hear bells! We had borrowed hand bells from a school which Earnie and I began to shake from the sleigh. David had fitted a spot light on his four wheel drive that beamed from the top of the hill. Of course, the closer we got down to the bottom, the more intense it became. The atmosphere was electric and the kids went wild!

Ernie's wife Edna made us Christmas waistcoats as we all dressed up as elves! Yes, what a sight! Money that was collected from the hash was used to purchase presents for the kids. They were graded into age groups and boy/girl, all wrapped up in festive paper. That was a job and a half for some lucky hashers' of an evening over a glass or two of 'juice'!

A tent was modified to use as a grotto and one of the hashers' did a great job at taking individual photos' of the children with Santa. The parents paid 5 riyals for the picture, (about one pound) to cover the cost of the film. An area was roped off so that the children lined up in an orderly line. There could be up to 400 people at a Christmas hash.

Once again, the camaraderie was fabulous! A lot of the ladies would make mince pies; mulled wine and sausage rolls. We even had a 'candy floss' machine which was a real treat for the kids. The choir from the British School would come out and sing carols and on one occasion, Simon, the music teacher from 'The Conti School' brought his electric keyboard out and the Goon Squad led the carols. We also sang a modified version of the twelve days of Christmas. Unfortunately we had misplaced the words so we got in touch with our good friend David Lewis, knowing that he would have archived the words. He didn't let us down, so here we go:

On the 1st day of Christmas my true love gave to me; A camel in a palm tree;

On the 2nd day; 2 Holy mosques;

On the 3rd day; 3 roast goats;

On the 4th day; 4 open sewers;

On the 5th day; 5 prayer calls;

On the 6th day; Mazda's crashing;

On the 7th day; Gosi refunds;

On the 8thday; sheik's a sleeping;

On the 9th day; Yemini's pooing;

On the 10th day; days in prison;

On the 11th day; trips to Makkah;

On the 12th; cops a kissing.

The whole event was a complete success and Ian, the GM was blown away .It became one of the best hash events of the year.

Owen and I would host a Christmas dinner for the committee at 'Flamingo' compound. We went out and bought extra cutlery, glasses and had green and red place mats made. We sat at tables decorated with crackers and hosted outside as the weather that time of year was the perfect temperature. There were usually about 22 people and we cooked a turkey, beef and an array of vegetables. Somebody would make a Christmas pudding and cake plus we had trifle, and a seasonal soup to start. There was also a 'secret Santa' gift, which you could try and win back if you lost the one that you particularly wanted! Great fun!

There were so many events with all the different groups that a calendar committee was formed to ensure that that functions didn't overlap.

'The Wizard of Oz' was another production that added to our repertoire. JLO put this famous musical on in conjunction with Jeddah Prep School. It was a huge production because the director wanted it to be as close to the original film as possible. If you recall, the opening of the film is in black and white, located on the farm in Kansas that belonged to Dorothy's guardians, Aunt Em and Uncle Henry. They don't have a particularly exciting life but Dorothy loves to dream and imagine life 'over the rainbow with her little dog Toto. A whirling cyclone lands her house in the land of 'Oz'. One weekend the cast involved met at the school at 6 a.m. before the sun came up. There was a wind machine to blow leaves for the cyclone and a rickety old shed to represent part of the farm. I played Aunty Em and Owen played Uncle Henry. On the evenings of the production a large screen was erected to portray the opening scene. It was done extremely well. My character in Oz was the good witch, Glinda and Owen played the guard in the tower that guarded 'The Emerald City'.

One evening I was watching the opening scene on a monitor in the dressing room and realised that I was due on NOW! The stage was in the gymnasium and JLO had paid for velvet curtains to be erected to correct the acoustics which meant that I had to run behind the curtains in the dark! The stage manager led me round and I can tell you the only word that came out of my mouth began with the letter F…! When I arrived on stage I could hardly get my lines out with all the huffing and puffing! And I had to sing! The next evening I waited in the wings before the show began to ensure that I was ready for my entrance.

CHAPTER 25 THE BEDOUINS, THE ARABIAN CAMEL,RACING AND PAGEANTS

In Jeddah there were a lot of empty apartment buildings that were built for the Bedouins. They remained empty because the Bedouins didn't want to give up their 'nomad' life in the desert to be cooped up in an apartment.

I'd like to tell you a bit about the Bedouin Arabs of Saudi Arabia because they are a very important part of its history and tradition.

The traditional homeland of the Bedouin Arab is the Arabian Desert, although some groups migrated into northern Africa. Saudi Arabia was one of the first lands inhabited by the Bedouin. It is said that almost 700,000 still live there. There are two main groups, the 'Rwala' and the 'Dhafir' but there is another group found mainly in southern Arabia known as the 'cattle' nomads or the 'Baggarah'.

The Bedouin represent two social classes. The first is the 'true' Bedouin who live as nomadic shepherds and the second are farmers known as the 'fellahin'.

The Bedouin Arab nomads live a challenging life and live in portable, black tents made from woven goat hair. The tents are divided with an ornamental partition called 'gata'. One half of the tent accommodates the women, children, cooking utensils and storage and the other contains a fireplace and is used by the males for entertaining.

The women do most of the work while the men socialize and make plans.

Bedouins don't have many possessions apart from their animals and tents due to their nomadic lifestyle. Goats and sheep are bought and sold whilst camels are their main source of transportation.

The main diet for Bedouins is dairy products and rice. Yogurt and butter is made from camel's milk, rice and unleavened bread when available. Dates are eaten for dessert as they are found in dessert oases. Meat is only eaten on special occasions.

Light-coloured and light weight clothing is worn due to the intense heat of the dessert. It is very loose-fitting to allow air circulation.

It was not the norm for Bedouins to undertake any kind of labour jobs but that has changed due to the need for better health conditions, more money and better living conditions. Some have accepted 'paying' jobs even though they may hate it.

Almost 100% of Bedouins in Saudi Arabia are 'Sunni Muslims'.

The Arabian camel, group name, 'Caravan flock' is a dromedary, which means it only has one hump. The hump can store up to 80 pounds of fat which the camel breaks down in to water and energy when food is not available. They also give the camel the ability to travel up to 100 desert miles without water even when temperatures reach 120 degrees F in the desert. Camels don't sweat until their body temperature reaches 106 degrees F and can drink 30 gallons of water in 13 minutes and conserve it for long periods of time. In winter, desert plants may hold enough moisture to allow the camel to survive without water for several weeks. The camel can reach 7 feet tall at the top of their hump, weigh up to 1,000 pounds and only eats plants.

Their nostrils close to keep sand from going up and they have bushy eyebrows and two rows of long eyelashes to protect their eyes. Their lips are large and tough to enable them to pick at dry and thorny desert vegetation. Big, thick footpads help them navigate the rough rocky terrain and shifting desert sands.

Arabian camels have been long valued as pack animals. They can carry large loads for up to 25 miles a day. A person's wealth can be based on the number of camels they own.

Unlike many other animals, camels move both legs on one side of the body at the same time.

Camel racing is one of the most traditional pastimes of the Arab world. Camel racing dates to the pre-Islamic area and the tradition of producing the strongest, fastest and most beautiful camels continues today.

A good racing camel is light weight and has small palms, a large chest, long legs and a long tail. These pampered contestants are fed a special diet of mostly dates, milk, honey, dry grass and corn, all super foods that help camels stay slim and trim. A healthy racing camel can run up to 40 kilometers in one hour on little water, so although they run at a slightly slower speed than horses, their endurance is second to none!

Beauty pageants are also very popular, especially in Riyadh during the month of February. In Riyadh it is part of the King Abdulaziz Camel Festival and can draw more than 30,000 well-groomed camels.

The contest is the highlight of the entire festival and showcases the dedication of camel handlers throughout Saudi Arabia. Camels are judged for their most graceful features, including the length of their necks, the shape of their noses, and of course, how they strut their stuff. Runway etiquette (and keeping a close eye out for cheaters) is essential during the camel beauty pageant, as the most gorgeous camels can fetch prizes up to a million Saudi riyals!

CHAPTER 26 PUNISHMENTS

Punishment in Saudi Arabia can be extremely severe but is taken very seriously, so I feel that it should be mentioned, although not dwelled upon.

Capital punishment is a legal penalty in Saudi Arabia when a murder is committed. An execution is usually carried out publicly by beheading the victim with a sword. Occasionally, the victim will be shot.

A murderer may be forgiven if 'blood money' is accepted by the family of the victim. The family can choose between execution, 'blood money' or forgiveness.

Other offences which result by death are:

- Apostasy, which in relation to Islam is conscious abandonment of Islam in word or through deed or converting to another religion if born into a Muslim family or if a non Muslim converts from another religion to Islam and then reverts back to their original religion.
- Drug trafficking
- Adultery; Women can be stoned to death or shot in the head if of a higher status.
- Witchcraft
- According to 'Sharia' law, certain other activities are prohibited; the consumption of alcohol and pork products, cross dressing and displays of affection in public.
- Theft; Depending on the circumstances, hand amputation from the wrist can be carried out.
- Assault; can be punished by beating.
- Violation of Islamic Law; Lashing could be administered, imprisonment or banishment, with_the victim being sent to another country or place.

CHAPTER 27 'SWAN SONGS' AND SAYING, 'GOODBYE'!

I was invited to attend an audition for 'Paddington Bear', with 'The Red Sea Players' group, which was being performed at The Greek Consulate. To my surprise, I was offered the part of 'Paddington'. I couldn't wait to begin rehearsals and worked very hard to get 'off script!' Chris, the director and I would rehearse independently from the other cast members to perfect Paddington's movements, gestures and facial expressions. It was also a musical so I had to dance and sing a song about marmalade. A friend of mine, Dot, made my costume from brown, fluffy car seat fabric which was extremely hot as I also had to wear the famous blue duffle coat, wellington boots and red, floppy hat. I had a very quick costume change into beach wear so Dot was waiting in the wings with the shorts opened ready for me to step into. The special effects were great; the washing machine shook furiously and overflowed with bubbles. There was a scene where I had to paint a room but of course everything went wrong. Tins of paint and a ladder were knocked over and a huge mess created! It was manic! At the end of each performance I would go out into the auditorium to greet the children. It was magical because they really did believe that I was Paddington. One little girl flung her arms around me and said, "I love you Paddington"! I was very touched and it was probably one of my best and memorable performances.

JLO put on a Christmas production of 'Scrooge' in conjunction with The American School. Owen was given the part of Scrooge and I was 'Tiny Tim's' mother. Owen was the first to be 'off script' which put the rest of us to shame! It was a magnificent production with singing, dancing and special effects involving the three ghosts played by very talented actors.

CHAPTER 28 SWAN SONGS AND SAYING GOODBYE!

Our 'swan song' was a production called 'It's all in the family', a farce written by Ray Coney. I played a matron in a hospital and Owen played a consultant. Jon, our friend and director of the show was insistent that he be present when I was measured for my uniform (an old fashioned one with the starched apron and arm bands). Why, you may ask yourself? Well, after being measured and unbeknown to me, Jon had the tailor take it in another 2 inches, which of course made it extremely tight and revealing! Mind you, it all added to my character, even though I kept trying to pull it down! There were some very funny scenes and some a little bit risqué but all in the name of comedy and good, old fashioned fun!

My father died in 2004 after a long and arduous illness. I had just returned from a vacation in the February on a British Airways, Wednesday evening flight which arrived on the Thursday morning and dad died the following morning. Owen had to request the help of a senior Saudi member of staff to help him acquire another exit/re-entry visa quickly so that I could go back out on the early Friday morning flight. When I boarded the return flight one of the attendants recognised me as it was the same crew that I had come in with. They were fabulous when they heard what had happened and insisted I sit up in first class, where they looked after me with genuine compassion and attention.

We had been in Saudi Arabia for twenty years (25 for Owen) and I was beginning to feel that I'd like to pursue another venture. I had always wanted to run my own B and B. but Owen wasn't totally on- board. Let's say he humoured me so we looked at some properties in Scotland on line. It was actually his sister, Elizabeth who found a property and emailed the details to us.

We decided to take a long weekend and go to Scotland to view it. We had only recently returned from a vacation but this was an important trip as we could have been making one of the biggest decisions of our lives! So we made arrangements to view the property and went back to Scotland. The property was on the main road to Dundee, in a small village called Fordelhill. The main house was two farm cottages joined together, made of stone. It was on one level with four double bedrooms all en-suite. There was a feature fireplace which separated the lounge from the dining area. The property was just under an acre which also housed a two bed wooden chalet and a two bed roomed, static caravan.

We both loved the property and saw the potential of it being a success so put an offer in (which was accepted) and change the course of our future!

We returned to Jeddah and began making plans to leave in March, 2005. We had to get Sam prepared for the journey as he had to be chipped 6 months before hand to avoid quarantine. We had a 'farewell party and reminisced over the past 20 years. A representative from Owen's company took us to the airport because at that time they had to supply the relevant exit only visa. We boarded the Air France flight with a little apprehension and Sam in tow. We were leaving the magical kingdom and coming out of the sand dunes to begin another chapter of our lives! Usually, they would weigh your cat because if it's over 5 kilos it has to be put in the 'hold' but luckily, they just asked his weight which was great because he was nearly 9 kilos! It meant that he could be put under our seat on the plane. It was a long journey as we had to touch down in Egypt for a couple of hours. Even though Sam had been given a sedative he began to stir, so I took him out of his carrier to cuddle and reassure him. We had put a small dog's harness on him for extra security. He settled back down but was a subject of conversation and stares amongst passengers' close by! We arrived in Paris approx 10 hours later. Why Paris I hear you say. Well, we had to take Sam to Calais to be checked by a vet that his chip was intact and legal. So the next part of our journey was to catch a train to Lille. As we were waiting on the station we decided to let Sam out of his carrier in case he wanted a 'wee'. Well, when we took him out and pulled back the floor of the carrier which had 'cat litter' in it, he produced the longest wee in the history of wees that ran the length of the platform. You could see the relief on his little face as he obviously didn't realize that he could have gone beforehand. We reached Calais in about two hours and checked into our hotel! Oh dear! I must tell you, Owen really surpassed himself this time! It was the most unusual shape because you had to climb a ladder to reach the bed and the settee and t.v. were underneath, like a child's bedroom with a bunk bed! The shower room was tucked into a corner but there was hardly anywhere to store the suitcases! Anyway, the more I think about it, the funnier it was. The next day we took Sam to the vet. It was a real wrench leaving him there but it was important that all the paper work and chip were in order. We found a bar that served good food, as the hotel wasn't up to much and it was walking distance. We visited Sam the next day just to let him know that mummy and daddy were still here and loved him. It was such a relief when we picked him up knowing that we could continue our journey to the UK with everything in order. The crossing on the ferry to Dover was without problems but unfortunately Sam had to be put in the hold so we didn't see him until we were in the arrivals hall when a animal handler handed him to us. It was a bit strange as we didn't actually go through customs with Sam; we just walked out of the building to the car rental office. We kept looking around as if we had done something wrong, like a criminal! The journey to Somerset was about a five hour drive so we decided to do it in a straight run, stopping a few times, mainly to give Sam a break. Before we reached Somerset, Helen had arranged with the land lord of the local B and B that Sam stay with us in the room, so we settled him there before meeting up with my sister. We stayed a couple of days and then headed up to Scotland in Rick and Helen's old BMW which we bought from them. It was an eight hour journey so we decided to break it up and stay in a 'welcome Inn'. We had to sneak Sam in as pets weren't allowed but it all added to the adventure because we also had to sneak him out!

It was quite an odd feeling arriving at our new abode, knowing that we would never return to a life that had brought us together and where we had opportunities unforgettable experiences.

So, thank-you Saudi Arabia for helping Owen and I live an extraordinary life. You will always have a special place in our hearts.

The End or is it?!

Printed in Great Britain
by Amazon

60654310R00059